Physical Characteristics of the Great Dane

(from the American Kennel Club breed standard)

W9-CNC-573

General Appearance: Regal appearance, dignity, strength and elegance with great size and a powerful, well-formed, smoothly muscled body.

Tail: Set high and smoothly into the croup, but not quite level with the back, a continuation of the spine. The tail should be broad at the base, tapering uniformly down to the hock joint.

Hindquarters: Strong, broad, muscular and well angulated, with well let down hocks. Seen from the rear, the hock joints appear to be perfectly straight, turned neither toward the inside nor toward the outside.

Coat: Short, thick and clean with a smooth glossy appearance.

Color: Markings and Patterns: Brindle, Fawn, Blue, Black, Harlequin, Mantle.

Size: Male shall not be less than 30 inches at the shoulders, but it is preferable that he be 32 inches or more, providing he is well proportioned to his height. The female shall not be less than 28 inches at the shoulders, but it is preferable that she be 30 inches or more, providing she is well proportioned to her height.

Feet: Round and compact with well-arched toes. The nails should be short, strong and as dark as possible, except that they may be lighter in harlequins.

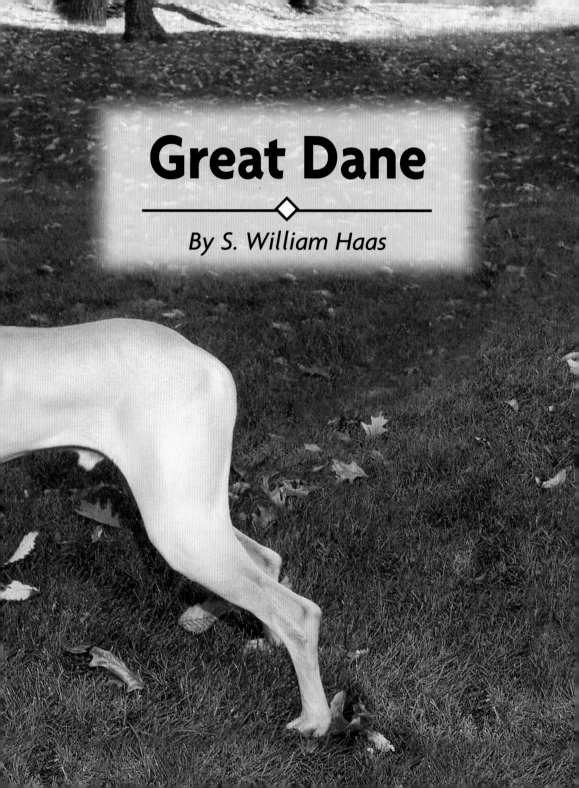

Great Dane

◇

By S. William Haas

Contents

KENNEL CLUB BOOKS® **GREAT DANE**
ISBN 13: 978-1-59378-273-3

Copyright © 2005, **2008** • Kennel Club Books® • A Division of BowTie, Inc.
40 Broad Street, Freehold, NJ 07728 USA
Cover Design Patented: US 6,435,559 B2 • Printed in South Korea

Photography by Isabelle Français and Carol Ann Johnson with additional photographs by:

Norvia Behling, T. J. Calhoun, Carolina Biological Supply, Doskocil, James R. Hayden, RBP, Bill Jonas, Dwight R. Kuhn, Dr. Dennis Kunkel, Mikki Pet Products, Phototake, Jean Claude Revy, Alice Roche and Dr. Andrew Spielman.

Illustrations by Patricia Peters and Renée Low.

The publisher wishes to thank Francisco Revelles Blanes, Donna Botte, Luis Rodriguez Cumplido, Leigh DeWitt, Dorothy W. Flood, Romana Förtsch, Robert Haltmeier, Tish Hamilton, Linda Kraft, Freda Lewis, Eric Marquard, Carol Mosher, Susan Nettleton, Lois Ostroski, G. & B. Pfaffenberger, Georgia Randall, Denise & Victor Rhodes, Werner & Inge Schorr, Nancy L. Simmons, Brigid M. Wiggins and Rob Wilson.

The "gentle giant" we know today as the Great Dane is a large, powerful, strong dog whose original purpose was hunting and fighting.

HISTORY OF THE
GREAT DANE

The mighty and powerful Great Dane was not always the "gentle giant" that it is often depicted and described as today. In fact, it was a very aggressive fighter and hunter that was terribly feared because of its harsh temperament and combative nature. Fortunately, through excellent breeding programs and dedicated fanciers, the breed has transformed over the years into a friendly and loving working dog that's suitable for families around the world.

Reports, artwork and artifacts indicate that a dog resembling the Great Dane might have existed over 2,000 years ago. It is believed that dogs similar to the Great Dane first belonged to one of the tribes of Asia called the Assyrians. The Assyrians used this ancient breed for hunting wild boar and other large game. The Great Dane's expert hunting skills allowed them to capture and kill these wild animals, which would later be used for food by the Asian people.

Although the Great Dane was originally bred for hunting and fighting, other tasks included carting, tracking and watchdog duties. Nonetheless, the breed was mainly kept as a showpiece for

This engraving from 1686 represents a wild boar hunt in Denmark. Early German writings called the breed the Danish Hound; it was in the 19th century that the Germans claimed the Great Dane as a national breed.

THE GERMAN INFLUENCE

We can be certain that the Great Dane first developed and flourished in Germany. In the 17th and 18th centuries, Germans imported Dane-like dogs, then called Boarhounds, upon which they based and established their own breeding programs. Throughout history, many influential dogs can be traced from German descent and today many winning pedigrees world-wide are still from German-bred dogs.

The breed's popularity increased throughout Germany when Prince Otto von Bismarck began housing many of them as his own personal pets. The breed first arrived in the German show ring in 1863, and the Deutsche

Prince Otto von Bismarck's love of the Great Dane furthered interest in the breed and its development in Germany.

Europe's ruling class. The breed was valued for its tremendous build, power, boldness and endurance. Today, it still possesses many of these same qualities. Some other accounts indicate that the Great Dane may have originated from a Mastiff-like dog that was present in England during the 1500s. The Greeks, Romans and Persians also kept these Mastiff-like dogs. Other theories defend the belief that the Tibetan Mastiff figures as strongly in the Dane's background as the English-type Mastiff. Like those of many other breeds, the Great Dane's origin is not entirely clear. There is no formal documentation that can definitively state its origins and development.

Doggen Club was formed in 1888. The club still exists today and is affiliated with the German VDH, which is the national association of dog breeders.

It was not until the late 1800s that the breed began migrating to other countries. One of the most famous German dogs of all time was Opal von Harlekin, a harlequin Great Dane bred by Herr Fuchs. Many of the Great Danes that are exhibited in Germany today continue to have the excellent conformation that their ancestors did hundreds of years ago. Fanciers of today owe a great debt to the early German breeders who concentrated on establishing type, focusing on such traits as color, size and, most importantly, sound temperament.

INTRODUCTION TO AMERICA

The first Great Dane ever recorded in America was a dog named "Prince" who was owned by Francis Butler of New York. As with Great Danes found in other countries at that time, the problem of poor temperaments was becoming more common. Dogs were extremely aggressive, and there were serious attempts to ban the breed completely. By 1889, breeders began making an honest attempt to improve the dogs' dispositions, and the first American breed club was formed. This club would later become the Great Dane Club of America.

EAR CROPPING

The Great Dane was originally used for the pursuit of wild boar and other large ferocious animals. Many dogs lost their lives while on these wild hunts, or returned with torn or mangled ears. Because of the frequent ear injuries associated with these hunts, removing ear flaps or ear cropping became a common practice. Ear cropping consists of surgically trimming the ear leathers and then training the ears to stand upright. In the US, dogs can be shown with cropped or natural ears, as is the case in most European nations, although it is more common to see cropped show dogs in the US. In the UK, however, ear cropping has been banned for years. American breeders concentrate on the stylish look of cropped ears, which they believe give the dog's head a more appealing, sharper look.

The beautiful head of Gazelle von Loheland of Ouborough, a Great Dane bitch bred in Germany in the 1930s.

The first Great Dane champion registered by the American Kennel Club was a German import named "Juno," who was owned by the Osceola kennel from Wisconsin. The Osceola kennel also owned Don Caesar, the second AKC champion, who won the very prestigious Westminster Kennel Club Dog Show in 1887.

During the 1920s and 1930s,

A modern-day Great Dane being shown in the UK, where ear cropping is banned.

many influential American dogs and breeders would emerge. Ch. Etfa von de Saalburg was considered to be one of the finest quality Great Danes ever bred, even by today's standards. The Walnut and Brae Tarn kennels were well respected. Some other top dogs of this era included Ch. Zorn v. Birknhof, Ch. Nero Hexengold and Ch. Czardus v. Eppelin Spring-Norris, who went on to sire ten champions. Another fine specimen was Ch. Ador Tipp Topp, who won Best in Show at Westminster in 1924.

Presently there are quite a few American kennels that have consistently produced quality dogs and it is an impossible task to list all of them. Some of the many fine kennels include Dagon, Rojon, Honey Lane, Von Rascac, Riverwood, Ranch, Warwick, Lincoln and Von Shrado.

HISTORY OF THE NAME

Before the Great Dane inherited the name that is widely recognized and accepted today, it was called many different things. Such names as German Mastiff, German Boarhound, English Dogge, Ulmer Dogge and Deutsche Dogge were common in countries around the world.

THE GREAT DANE IN THE UNITED KINGDOM

The breed's popularity in England was slow at first, but would change as the years went by. During the late 19th century, a

The Great Dane of yesteryear resembles today's breed in physical conformation, but the modern Dane's temperament is nothing like his aggressive ancestors.

rabies scare swept the country and many dogs were destroyed.

Originally, the Great Dane in the UK was referred to as the German Boarhound and was considered to be a sporting dog. It was not until 1894 that the name was changed to Great Dane in the English Stud Book. The first breed classes began at the Alexandra Palace show in January 1879. The breed would eventually begin to grow in popularity. In 1883, the Great Dane Club was formed. Mr. Adcock, who was a great admirer of the breed, headed the club. Mr. Petrzywalski's Ch. Sultan II became the first champion in the breed in 1884.

What a sight—a photo from an obedience exhibition in the 1930s that featured 100 Great Danes! None of the dogs is aggressive or shows any signs of disinterest. All of the dogs belonged to Gordon Stewart, owner of the Send kennels.

Mrs. J. Arthur Rank with four great dogs from the Ouborough kennel, all of which were champions.

"BOUNCE" SAVES POET

The popular 18th-century poet, Alexander Pope was a great admirer of the Great Dane. In fact, his dog Bounce saved his life one evening when a servant attempted to slay him. The servant broke into Pope's quarters and tried to stab him. Springing to his master's defense, Bounce attacked the intruder and prevented what could have been a savage murder.

In 1895, The Kennel Club's banning of ear cropping would have a great impact on the breed's reputation in the country. This ruling angered many English Great Dane breeders. It discouraged many individuals from becoming active or involved in the breed, and several withdrew from the fancy because of it.

Despite the ear-cropping ban, many English breeders eventu-

ally developed reputable breeding programs that had a great influence on the breed. Violet Horsfall and her Redgraves kennel was one of the most influential English kennels of the time. Some of her famous dogs included English Champions Viola, Therr, Hannibel of Redgrave and Viceroy of Redgrave, who completed his show career with 21 Challenge

Eng. Ch. Maurice of Cuddington, born in August of 1923, started winning in 1924 and won his last show in 1930, never missing a year.

His Royal Highness Prince George with the beautiful Great Dane, Ch. Midas.

War I, can still be found in top dogs in Great Britain today.

World War II affected the breeding of Great Danes even more severely than World War I. The breed suffered tremendously and nearly became extinct once again. However, dedicated breeders kept the breed going, and the Great Dane regained its foothold and remains that way today.

The Great Dane continues to be alive and well in Great Britain. The devotion towards the breed is strong and many kennels have made a name for themselves in the breed. Some of the more prominent include Endroma, Garask, Yacanto and Nightgifts.

Certificates to his credit. Many people considered Violet Horsfall to be the pioneer breeder of the modern Great Dane in England. In addition, the Ouborough and Send prefixes, essential in reviving the breed after World

These two dogs, named "Hannibal" and "Princess," arrived from Germany in 1807 and were presented to HRH the Duchess of York. They were classified as "Wildboar Hounds of the Second Class" or "Tiger-dogs."

CHARACTERISTICS OF THE
GREAT DANE

IS THE GREAT DANE THE RIGHT DOG FOR YOU?

Even if you've decided that you are ready for the responsibilities and hard work associated with dog ownership, choosing what type of dog is right for you is never easy. Many things must be taken into consideration. Do you have the space for a dog, more specifically a dog the size of the Great Dane? Do you have the time required to train the dog and provide him with the love and companionship he requires? Do you have the financial resources to care for and feed a Great Dane?

Having answered yes to all of these questions, it's time to begin the exciting and fulfilling search for that special puppy or adult

dog. If you've chosen the Great Dane, you've made an excellent selection that I'm sure won't disappoint you. Trustworthy, loyal and dependable, the Great Dane is an awesome companion and friend. Once you have chosen a Great Dane as your own, you have gained a faithful friend for life. The Great Dane is a marvelous family companion who loves children and adults alike. The breed adjusts easily to the home envi-

The Great Dane is a canine friend beyond compare for the right owner.

TAKING CARE

Science is showing that as people take care of their pets, the pets are taking care of their owners. A recent study published in the *American Journal of Cardiology* found that having a pet can prolong his owner's life. Pet owners generally have lower blood pressure, and pets help their owners to relax and keep more physically fit. It was also found that pets help to keep the elderly connected to their communities.

ronment and quickly bonds with his new family members. The Great Dane loves attention and will be very unhappy if he doesn't receive the love and admiration of his family. This is truly a people's dog.

The majestic appeal of the Great Dane is acknowledged world-wide. Most people are familiar with the breed and many have known a family member or friend who has owned one. The general public loves the breed's giant size and regal demeanor; the breed seems to have an instant appeal to people. Once you have seen its magnificent size and beauty up close, the very sight of the Great Dane is rather breathtaking and memorable.

Great Danes develop a gentle affection for children... and vice versa.

Most people who decide to purchase a Great Dane will have the breed for life. New dog owners immediately develop a strong bond and fondness for the breed. Rarely will a Great Dane owner switch to a different breed once he has owned one, and he will more likely add another Great Dane to his household!

THE GREAT DANE AS A GUARD DOG

It can't be stressed enough how much of a family dog the Great Dane really is. Once the dog has determined who his lucky family members are, and has adjusted to his new living surroundings, he will sacrifice himself for the safety and welfare of his loved ones. Because of their strong love for family members, Great Danes don't take well to strangers. It will usually take some time before the Great Dane warms to people that he does not know.

There is absolutely no question that the Great Dane is a very intimidating breed. The very sight of one can be a frightening experience for anyone. Although they can be very standoffish to people that they don't know, this should not be taken as a negative trait. The dog is only doing what he feels is his job—to protect his family at all costs.

The Great Dane has a very loud, fierce-sounding bark that will usually discourage strangers or intruders from invading one's private property or home. Usually, the dog's mammoth size is enough to frighten any person who is senseless enough to challenge him or his family.

Although the Great Dane serves well as a guard dog, his bold appearance should not cause him to be mistaken for an aggressive animal. The breed is very loving and most of them wouldn't harm a hookworm! Yet, if they are provoked, they will defend themselves and their family.

CHOOSING A PUPPY OR AN ADULT GREAT DANE

Deciding on a Great Dane puppy or an adult Great Dane is never an easy decision. There are advantages and disadvantages to both. Acquiring a young puppy allows the owner to mold his new dog to adapt to a functioning living pattern that easily fits the owner's specific lifestyle. An older dog is usually set in his ways and can be difficult to break of old habits. You must keep in mind that even the Great Dane puppy will be considerably large and will require enough space for adequate training and socialization.

Whether you choose a puppy or an adult dog, the Great Dane adjusts quickly to his new home. The puppy's love and desire for family companionship quickly overcome his short-term fear of leaving his littermates and mother

NORMAL FOOD INTAKE
Because of the breed's massive size, many uninformed potential Great Dane owners believe that the breed requires massive amounts of food. The truth is quite the contrary. Despite their large frame, the adult Great Dane eats no more than the average-sized dog. On the other hand, the Great Dane youngster requires a substantial amount of food to support his growing body.

behind for the first time, or, in the case of an adult, leaving his former home for an unfamiliar place. The puppy develops his independence rather quickly and will look to his new owner(s) for the affection and support he so desperately needs. The Great Dane will most likely emulate the personalities of his new owners. Therefore, it's up to you how well adjusted your youngster or adult dog will become.

THE SEARCH FOR THAT PERFECT DOG

Contacting a reputable Great Dane breeder may require some work and research on your part. Depending on your location, finding a puppy or adult may be either relatively easy or somewhat difficult. A good way to start is by contacting Great Dane or all-breed clubs near your home. You can also contact the AKC and ask for a list of Great Dane breeders in your area. Another good place to search for reputable Great Dane contacts is a dog show. Acquire a list of shows and make plans to attend. Many reputable breeders and Great Dane experts can be found at dog shows. If you introduce yourself politely, and express your sincere interest in the breed, most Great Dane fanciers will be happy to spend the time answering your questions concerning the breed. If you have the time, watch the Great Danes being exhibited at the show. A tremendous amount can be learned by watching a large class

Finding a good breeder of Great Danes is not easy, but when you do you will know immediately. A dedicated breeder will *live* Great Danes!

of Great Danes being judged. Take notes. Learn to develop an eye for the breed, and mark down the types of dogs you think you may be interested in. Then, after the exhibiting is complete, introduce yourself to the handlers and people associated with the dogs that caught your eye.

PET OR SHOW DOG?

Once you have made some reliable contacts, you should make plans to visit some Great Dane kennels. You should decide what type of dog you are looking for, and what you intend to do with him. Are you interested in competing in the show ring or possibly obedience? Or, are you simply looking for a Great Dane that is healthy and has an excellent temperament and pedigree? Make sure to inform the Great Dane breeders you visit of your intentions. This will help them select a puppy or dog that is just right for you and your family.

Keep in mind that a reputable Great Dane breeder will be well versed in what to look for in choosing a new puppy or adult. Take his advice. The breeder will know how his own bloodline develops, and should be willing and able to point out both the good and bad points of his individual line. You should ask to see the sire and dam of the litter if they are on the kennel's premises. Do the puppies' parents look

SKILLFUL MANEUVERING
Despite their huge size, Great Danes have a unique ability that enables them to stay out of the way of family traffic in the home. Frequently, they can be found bunched up in a ball, lounging on the family's couch or living room floor. They are not as clumsy as one would think, but are actually quite skillful in maneuvering safely through tight quarters.

healthy and happy? Are the puppies outgoing and do they appear well cared for?

The price of a Great Dane will vary from breeder to breeder and region to region. Obviously, a potential show puppy will cost more than a pet. Frequently, many people will ask what the difference is between choosing a bitch or a dog, and if the price for each varies. In Great Danes, bitches are usually more gentle in temperament and are a bit more loving. Obviously, if you decide to purchase a bitch, you will have to deal with the fact that she will likely come into season twice a year. This can be a major inconvenience if you have male dogs on your property that have not been neutered. Of course, the breeder should require you to spay or neuter the pup if it is not a potential show or breeding dog. The male Great Dane will be considerably larger than the female and will often appeal to those individuals looking for a dog with bigger bone and mass. The price for both sexes is about the same. Great Danes have such large litters that the value for each sex remains fairly stable. If you decide to purchase a harlequin-colored dog, expect to pay more because the color is rarer than some others.

HOW MUCH EXERCISE IS ENOUGH?

The Great Dane is a powerful working dog that was originally bred to hunt large wild game hundreds of years ago. By today's requirements and expectations, the breed doesn't need as much exercise as its size might suggest. In fact, the Great Dane does not require any more exercise than a regular-sized dog. If you have the time to take him on some long daily walks, or for a brief run in a field or park, that should suffice. As long as your Great Dane gets to stretch his long, sturdy legs daily, he will receive the necessary exercise requirements. Combining a good feeding program and exercise will ensure a healthy, attrac-

Despite its large size, the Great Dane does not require more exercise than a regular-sized dog. Activity is, however, necessary— long daily walks or off-leash runs in a secure area will suffice to give your adult Great Dane the exercise he needs.

tive dog. Remember never to overdo exercise with a developing puppy, as strenuous exercise can have long-lasting adverse effects on a puppy's growing ligaments and bones.

THE GREAT DANE'S HEALTH CONCERNS

Every dog owner's goal is to try and keep his dog as happy and healthy as possible. Fortunately, the Great Dane is a very healthy breed of dog. On the whole, they have very few health problems of which an owner needs to be aware. Provided that you have purchased your dog from a reputable breeder who tests for problems and breeds only healthy dogs, everything should be fine. The breeder should provide a health certificate from his own veterinarian indicating that his stock has been thoroughly checked and are in optimum health. You should also receive a record of your chosen dog's worming shots. You can bring this record along with you to your own vet's office. In all cases, it's recommended that you have your own veterinarian examine the dog very soon after you have purchased him and have him home.

BLOAT (GASTRIC TORSION)

Bloat is a condition that affects large and deep-chested breeds. It can occur in smaller dogs, but larger breeds are more susceptible.

Great Dane owners must be aware of this very serious condition that involves the release of gas from food in the dog's stomach, which

DOGS, DOGS, GOOD FOR YOUR HEART!

People usually purchase dogs for companionship, but studies show that dogs can help to improve their owners' health and level of activity, as well as lower a human's risk of coronary heart disease. Without even realizing it, when a person puts time into exercising, grooming and feeding a dog, he also puts more time into his own personal health care. Dog owners establish more routine schedules for their dogs to follow, which can have positive effects on their own health. Dogs also teach us patience, offer unconditional love and provide the joy of having a furry friend to pet!

eventually causes the stomach to twist and turn, cutting off the blood supply and preventing gas and stomach contents from leaving. What makes the condition so serious is that you never know when bloat is going to occur. When it does, there is very little time to seek veterinary care. If the dog isn't rushed into surgery immediately, he likely will die.

HOW TO PREVENT BLOAT

Research has confirmed that the structure of deep-chested breeds contributes to their predisposition to bloat. Nevertheless, there are precautions that you can take to reduce the risk.

- Feed your dog twice daily rather than offer one big meal.
- Do not exercise your dog for at least one hour before and two hours after he has eaten.
- Make certain that your dog is calm and not overly excited while he is eating. It has been proven that nervous or overly excited dogs are more prone to develop bloat.
- Add a small portion of moist meat product to his dry food ration.
- Serve his meals and water in an elevated bowl stand, which avoids the dog's craning his neck.
- To prevent your dog from gobbling his food too quickly, and thereby swallowing air, put some large (unswallowable) toys into his bowl so that he will have to eat around them to get his food.
- Never let your dog gulp water.

FOREIGN OBJECTS AND POISONOUS SUBSTANCES

Great Dane puppies can be very curious. Their curiosity can sometimes get them into serious trouble. It's not uncommon for them to pick up rocks or other foreign substances off the ground. In doing so, they may swallow something that is extremely harmful, if not deadly. It's important to keep any small objects, poisonous liquids, detergents or cleaning fluids out of both the young and adult dog's reach. Keep in mind that the Great Dane is larger than most other breeds, and is therefore fully capable of reaching places that ordinary-sized dogs could not.

If you suspect that your Great Dane has swallowed something foreign, induce vomiting at once. Placing peroxide or washing soda in the dog's mouth will force the dog to vomit, and hopefully discharge any foreign substance or liquid he has swallowed. Immediately contact your veterinarian for further assistance.

TEENAGE SPOTS

This is a condition that causes harmless black or brown spots to appear around the mouth and below the dog's chin. There is no need to panic if your Great Dane develops such symptoms. Although the cause of these spots is unknown, they will disappear in time.

HEART PROBLEMS

Great Danes may be susceptible to a serious heart muscle condition known as dilated cardiomyopathy, which eventually causes heart failure. This form of heart muscle defect is common in large breeds such as the Great Dane, Doberman Pinscher and German Shepherd, as well as some of the spaniel breeds. The affected heart is unable to pump properly due to its stretched condition. The cause is quite unknown, though a genetic predisposition is suggested as is a nutritional amino-acid imbalance (which has been observed in the Boxer and Doberman Pinscher). Early signs in the Great Dane include coughing, general weakness and depression, and decreased interest in food and exercise, plus the possibility of an increased heart rate. Sudden deaths have been recorded in many cases of the defect in the Great Dane.

WOBBLER SYNDROME

Wobbler syndrome is a serious disease that is caused by the compression of the spinal cord, which in turn causes the neck bone to be disfigured. Dogs that are affected with the condition usually cannot support the weight of their rear end, and have a drunken-like movement. It usually develops in dogs that are three to five months of age. Although surgery is available to treat the condition, most attempts are not successful. The disease is inherited, and any dog that has the condition should be immediately removed from any breeding program.

HEAT STROKE

Heat stroke is the number-one summer-related cause of death in dogs. Year after year, despite all the information that's printed in newspapers and displayed on television, negligent dog owners insist on overheating their dogs in hot, sun-baked cars or yards. The Great Dane can tolerate warm weather quite well, but must not be exposed to excessive heat for long periods of time. If your Great Dane appears to be suffering from heat stroke, administer cold ice packs immediately and get him to a cool location at once. Large breeds of dog, such as the Great Dane, will usually get much warmer more quickly than smaller dogs.

DO YOU KNOW ABOUT HIP DYSPLASIA?

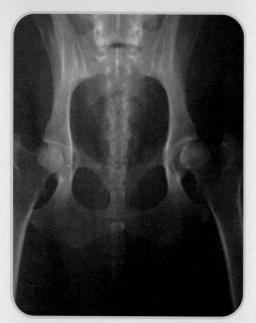

Above: X-ray of a dog with "Good" hips.

X-ray of a dog with "Moderate" dysplastic hips.

Hip dysplasia is a fairly common condition found in pure-bred dogs. When a dog has hip dysplasia, his hind leg has an incorrectly formed hip joint. By constant use of the hip joint, it becomes more and more loose, wears abnormally and may become arthritic.

Hip dysplasia can only be confirmed with an x-ray, but certain symptoms may indicate a problem. Your dog may have a hip dysplasia problem if he walks in a peculiar manner, hops instead of smoothly runs, uses his hind legs in unison (to keep the pressure off the weak joint), has trouble getting up from a prone position or always sits with both legs together on one side of his body.

As the dog matures, he may adapt well to life with a bad hip, but in a few years the arthritis develops and many dogs with hip dysplasia become crippled.

Hip dysplasia is considered an inherited disease and only can be diagnosed definitively when the dog is two years old. Some experts claim that a special diet might help your puppy outgrow the bad hip, but the usual treatments are surgical. The removal of the pectineus muscle, the removal of the round part of the femur, reconstructing the pelvis and replacing the hip with an artificial one are all surgical interventions that are expensive, but they are usually successful. Follow the advice of your veterinarian.

HIP DYSPLASIA

Hip dysplasia is a well-known condition that affects many hunting, herding and working breeds. It affects either one or both hip joints, and is a result of looseness, or improper fit, of the ball and socket. The condition can be inherited or caused by a quick weight gain in younger dogs. Although surgery is available to correct the condition, most procedures are very expensive and may not always be successful. Puppies can be tested, but not until 24 months of age can a dog be diagnosed with or cleared as free of the condition. Dogs that test positive through x-rays should not be used in one's breeding program.

ENTROPION/ECTROPION

Although not very common, entropion does occur in Great Danes. The ailment involves the inward turning of the eyelid, which results in the eyelashes' scratching the surface of the eyeball. It can be a very painful condition that may eventually lead to corneal ulceration. Fortunately, treatment is available through a veterinarian.

In the condition known as ectropion, the lower eyelid turns outwards. The end result is usually severe eye irritation (redness, soreness, etc.) and possible infection and discharge. This inherited condition can also be treated by ointments and antibiotics administered by your veterinarian.

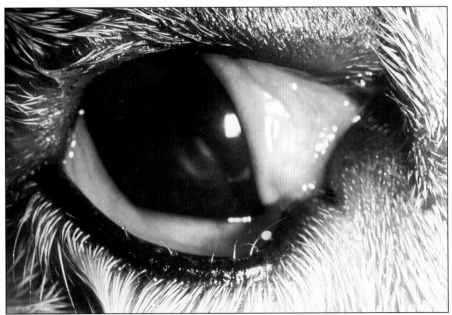

Lower entropion, or rolling in of the eyelid, is causing irritation in the eye shown. Several extra eyelashes, or distichiasis, are present on the lower lid.

BREED STANDARD FOR THE
GREAT DANE

THE SIGNIFICANCE OF THE BREED STANDARD

The breed standard is an attempt to describe what the "ideal" specimen of a particular breed should look like. Although no such dog will ever exist, the breed standard is a valuable guideline used by exhibitors, judges, breeders and other Great Dane fanciers. It helps them understand the qualities that they should be looking for when buying, judging or breeding a dog.

Referring and adhering to the breed standard on a regular basis helps to keep the breed's defining characteristics alive and well. Without it, the breed would eventually change. Unfortunately, like most things, the breed standard is not perfect and can vary slightly from country to country. It's open to a great deal of interpretation that can easily be misunderstood by individuals who are just getting started in the breed. Nevertheless, the breed standard is very important and must be treated as the exhibitor's, breeder's and judge's bible.

The general appearance of the Great Dane must be that of a muscular dog, strongly but elegantly built.

THE AMERICAN KENNEL CLUB BREED STANDARD FOR THE GREAT DANE

GENERAL APPEARANCE

The Great Dane combines, in its regal appearance, dignity, strength and elegance with great size and a powerful, well-formed, smoothly muscled body. It is one of the giant working breeds, but is unique in that its general conformation must be so well balanced that it never appears clumsy, and shall move with a long reach and powerful drive. It is always a unit—the Apollo of dogs. A Great Dane must be spirited, courageous, never timid; always friendly and dependable. This physical and mental combination is the characteristic which gives the Great Dane the majesty possessed by no other breed. It is particularly true of this breed that there is an impression of great masculinity in dogs, as compared to an impression of femininity in bitches. Lack of true Dane breed type, as defined in this standard, is a serious fault.

SIZE, PROPORTION, SUBSTANCE

The male should appear more massive throughout than the bitch, with larger frame and heavier bone. In the ratio between length and height, the Great Dane should be square. In bitches, a somewhat longer body is permissible, providing she is well proportioned to her height. Coarseness or lack of substance are equally undesirable. The male shall not be less than 30 inches at the shoulders, but it is preferable that he be 32 inches or more, providing he is well proportioned to his height. The female shall not be less than 28 inches at the shoulders, but it is preferable that she be 30 inches or more,

providing she is well proportioned to her height. Danes under minimum height must be disqualified.

HEAD

The head shall be rectangular, long, distinguished, expressive, finely chiseled, especially below the eyes. Seen from the side, the Dane's forehead must be sharply set off from the bridge of the nose, (a strongly pronounced stop). The plane of the skull and the plane of the muzzle must be straight and parallel to one another. The skull plane under and to the inner point of the eye must slope without any bony protuberance in a smooth line to a full square jaw with a deep muzzle (fluttering lips are undesirable). The masculinity of the male is very pronounced in structural appearance of the head. The bitch's head is more delicately formed. Seen from the top, the skull should have parallel sides and the bridge of the nose

BREEDER'S BLUEPRINT

If you are considering breeding your bitch, it is very important that you are familiar with the breed standard. Reputable breeders breed with the intention of producing dogs that are as close as possible to the standard and that contribute to the advancement of the breed. Study the standard for both physical appearance and temperament, and make certain your bitch and your chosen stud dog measure up.

The head should give an overall rectangular impression, long with flat planes, all in proportion.

should be as broad as possible. The cheek muscles should not be prominent. The length from the tip of the nose to the center of the stop should be equal to the length from the center of the stop to the rear of the slightly developed occiput. The head should be angular from all sides and should have flat planes with dimensions in proportion to the size of the Dane. Whiskers may be trimmed or left natural.

Eyes shall be medium size, deep set, and dark, with a lively intelligent expression. The eyelids are almond-shaped and relatively tight, with well developed brows. Haws and mongolian eyes are serious faults. In harlequins, the eyes should be dark; light colored eyes, eyes of different colors and walleyes are permitted but not desirable.

Ears shall be high set, medium in size and of moderate thickness, folded forward close to the cheek. The top line of the folded ear should be level with the skull. If cropped, the ear length is in proportion to the size of the head and the ears are carried uniformly erect.

Nose shall be black, except in the blue Dane, where it is a dark blue-black. A black spotted nose is permitted on the harlequin; a pink colored nose is not desirable. A split nose is a disqualification.

Teeth shall be strong, well developed, clean and with full dentition. The incisors of the lower jaw touch very lightly the bottoms of the inner surface of the upper incisors (scissors bite). An undershot jaw is a very serious fault. Overshot or wry bites are serious faults. Even bites, mis-aligned or crowded incisors are minor faults.

NECK, TOPLINE, BODY

The neck shall be firm, high set, well arched, long and muscular. From the nape, it should gradually broaden and flow smoothly into the withers. The neck under-line should be clean. Withers shall slope smoothly into a short level back with a broad loin. The chest shall be broad, deep and well muscled. The forechest should be well developed without a pronounced sternum. The brisket extends to the elbow, with well sprung ribs. The body underline should be tightly muscled with a well-defined tuck-up.

The croup should be broad and very slightly sloping. The tail should be set high and smoothly into the croup, but not quite level with the back, a continuation of the spine. The tail should be broad at the base, tapering uniformly down to the hock joint. At rest, the tail should fall straight. When excited or running, it may curve slightly, but never above the level of the back. A ring or hooked tail is a serious fault. A docked tail is a disqualification.

FOREQUARTERS

The forequarters, viewed from the side, shall be strong and muscular. The shoulder blade must be strong and sloping, forming, as near as possible, a right angle in its articulation with the upper arm. A line from the upper tip of the shoulder to the back of the elbow joint should be perpendicular. The ligaments and muscles holding the shoulder blade to the rib cage must be well developed, firm and securely attached to prevent loose shoulders. The shoulder blade and the upper arm should be the same length. The elbow should be one-half the

MEETING THE IDEAL

The American Kennel Club defines a standard as "A description of the ideal dog of each recognized breed, to serve as an ideal against which dogs are judged at shows." This "blueprint" is drawn up by the breed's recognized parent club, approved by a majority of its membership, and then submitted to the AKC for approval.

The AKC states that "An understanding of any breed must begin with its standard. This applies to all dogs, not just those intended for showing." The picture that the standard draws of the dog's type, gait, temperament and structure is the guiding image used by breeders as they plan their programs.

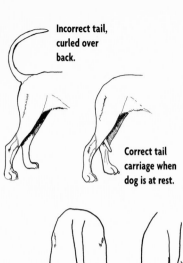

Incorrect tail, curled over back.

Correct tail carriage when dog is at rest.

Cropped ears are proportionate to head and erect.

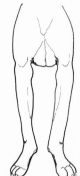

Natural ears are medium-sized and folded close to cheeks.

Correct hindquarters.

Poor hocks, turning in.

Correct straight forequarters.

Incorrect forequarters, feet turning out.

FAULTS IN PROFILE

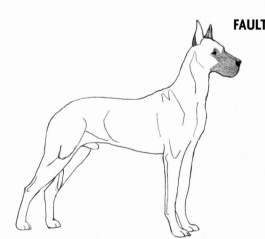

Ewe-necked, upright shoulders, dip in topline behind withers, weak pasterns, flat feet, shallow chested, lacking sufficient angulation in rear.

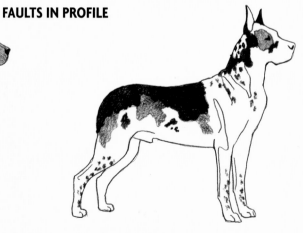

Short bull neck, loaded shoulders, long back, soft topline, short muzzle, steep croup and weak rear, faults in harlequin markings with large merle patches, Dalmatian-type spotting, large blanket, unpigmented nose.

Profile showing ideal type, balance and structure.

distance from the withers to the ground. The strong pasterns should slope slightly. The feet should be round and compact with well-arched toes, neither toeing in, toeing out, nor rolling to the inside or outside. The nails should be short, strong and as dark as possible, except that they may be lighter in harlequins. Dewclaws may or may not be removed.

HINDQUARTERS
The hindquarters shall be strong, broad, muscular and well angulated, with well let down hocks.

Seen from the rear, the hock joints appear to be perfectly straight, turned neither toward the inside nor toward the outside. The rear feet should be round and compact, with well-arched toes, neither toeing in nor out. The nails should be short, strong and as dark as possible, except they may be lighter in harlequins. Wolf claws are a serious fault.

COAT
The coat shall be short, thick and clean with a smooth glossy appearance.

The Great Dane's jaw is full and square, with full dention in a scissors bite.

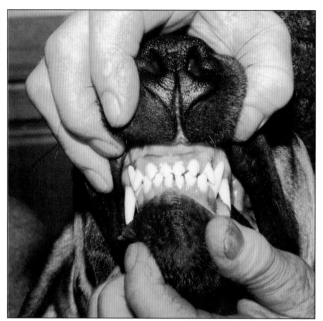

COLOR, MARKINGS AND PATTERNS

Brindle—The base color shall be yellow gold and always brindled with strong black cross stripes in a chevron pattern. A black mask is preferred. Black should appear on the eye rims and eyebrows, and may appear on the ears and tail tip. The more intensive the base color and the more distinct and even the brindling, the more preferred will be the color. Too much or too little brindling are equally undesirable. White markings at the chest and toes, black-fronted, dirty colored brindles are not desirable.

Fawn—The color shall be yellow gold with a black mask. Black should appear on the eye rims and eyebrows, and may appear on the ears and tail tip. The deep yellow gold must always be given the preference. White markings at the chest and toes, black-fronted dirty colored fawns are not desirable.

Blue—The color shall be a pure steel blue. White markings at the chest and toes are not desirable.

Black—The color shall be a glossy black. White markings at the chest and toes are not desirable.

Harlequin—Base color shall be pure white with black torn patches irregularly and well distributed over the entire body; a pure white neck is preferred. The black patches should never be large enough to give the appearance of a blanket, nor so small as to give a stippled or dappled effect. Eligible, but less desirable, are a few small gray patches, or a white base with single black hairs showing through, which tend to give a salt and pepper or dirty effect.

Mantle—The color shall be black and white with a solid black blanket extending over the body; black skull with white muzzle;

GAIT

The gait denotes strength and power with long, easy strides resulting in no tossing, rolling or bouncing of the topline or body. The backline shall appear level and parallel to the ground. The long reach should strike the ground below the nose while the head is carried forward. The powerful rear drive should be balanced to the reach. As speed increases, there is a natural tendency for the legs to converge toward the centerline of balance beneath the body. There should be no twisting in or out at the elbow or hock joints.

white blaze is optional; whole white collar is preferred; a white chest; white on part or whole of forelegs and hind legs; white tipped black tail. A small white marking in the blanket is acceptable, as is a break in the white collar.

Any variance in color or markings as described above shall be faulted to the extent of the deviation. Any Great Dane which does not fall within the above color classifications must be disqualified.

TEMPERAMENT

The Great Dane must be spirited, courageous, always friendly and dependable, and never timid or aggressive.

DISQUALIFICATIONS

Danes under minimum height.
Split nose. Docked Tail.
Any color other than those described under "Color, Markings and Patterns."

Standard approved March 8, 1999
Effective April 28, 1999

PUPPY'S PAPERS

Too often new owners are confused between two important documents. Your puppy's pedigree, essentially a family tree, is a written record of a dog's genealogy of three generations or more. The pedigree will show you the names as well as performance titles of all the dogs in your pup's background. Your breeder must provide you with a registration application, with his part properly filled out. You must complete the application and send it to the American Kennel Club with the proper fee. The American Kennel Club requires that the seller provide the buyer with the following: breed; sex, color and markings; date of birth; litter number (when available); names and registration numbers of the parents; breeder's name; and date sold or delivered.

If you have acquired a puppy and have no interest in showing or breeding, you can apply for an ILP or Indefinite Listing Privilege, which affords your dog the opportunity to participate in obedience, agility, tracking and many other performance events. An ILP does not replace the dog's registration certification, and all ILPs must belong to an AKC-recognized breed and be spayed or neutered.

WHERE TO BEGIN?

If you are convinced that the Great Dane is the ideal dog for you, it's time to learn about where to find a puppy and what to look for. Locating a litter of Great Danes will require some research, but you'll likely be able to find a good breeder within a reasonable distance from your home. You should inquire about breeders who enjoy a good reputation in the breed. You are looking for an established breeder with outstanding dog ethics and a strong commitment to the breed. New owners should have as many questions as they have doubts. An established breeder is indeed the one to answer your four million questions and make you comfortable with your choice of the Great Dane. An established breeder will sell you a puppy at a fair price if, and only if, the breeder determines that you are a suitable, worthy owner of his dogs. An established breeder can be relied upon for advice, no matter what time of day or night. A reputable breeder will accept a puppy back, without questions, if health problems arise or if you should decide that this is not the right dog for you.

When choosing a breeder, reputation is much more important than convenience of location. Do not be overly impressed by breeders who run brag advertisements in the dog publications about their stupendous champions. The real quality breeders are quiet and unassuming. You hear about them at dog shows and trials, by word of mouth. You may be well advised to avoid the novice who lives only a couple of miles away. The novice breeder, trying so hard to get rid of that first litter of puppies, is more than accommodating and anxious to sell you one. That breeder will charge you as much as any established breeder. The novice breeder isn't going to interrogate you and your family about your intentions with the puppy, the environment and training you can provide, etc. That breeder will be nowhere to be found when your poorly bred, badly adjusted four-pawed monster starts to growl and spit up at midnight or eat the family cat!

While health considerations and eliminating hereditary problems in the Great Dane are the breeder's first concern, socialization is another breeder concern of immense importance. Since the Great Dane's temperament can vary from line to line, early socialization is the best way to encour-

TEMPERAMENT COUNTS

Your selection of a good puppy can be determined by your needs. A show potential or a good pet? It is your choice. Every puppy, however, should be of good temperament. Although show-quality puppies are bred and raised with emphasis on physical conformation, responsible breeders strive for equally good temperament. Do not buy from a breeder who concentrates solely on physical beauty at the expense of personality.

age proper stable personalities in the developing puppies.

Once you have contacted and met a breeder or two and made your choice about which breeder is best suited to your needs, it's time to visit the litter. Keep in mind that many top breeders have waiting lists. Sometimes new owners have to wait a year or more for a puppy. If you are really committed to the breeder whom

PUPPY APPEARANCE

Your puppy should have a well-fed appearance but not a distended abdomen, which may indicate worms or incorrect feeding, or both. The body should be firm, with a solid feel. The skin of the abdomen should be pale pink and clean, without signs of scratching or rash. Dewclaws may or may not be removed; check to see if the breeder has done this, as it is usually done at a very young age.

you've selected, then you will wait (and hope for an early arrival!). If not, you may have to resort to your second- or third-choice breeder. Don't be too anxious, however. If the breeder doesn't have any waiting list, or any customers, there is probably a good reason. It's no different than visiting a restaurant with no clientele. The better restaurants always have a waiting list—and it's usually worth the wait. Besides, isn't a puppy more important than a meal?

Since you are likely to be choosing a Great Dane as a pet dog and not a show dog, you simply should select a pup that is healthy, friendly and attractive. Great Danes generally have large litters, averaging eight to ten puppies, so you will usually have a wide selection once you have located a desirable litter.

If you want your new charge to compete in dog shows, there are many more considerations. The parents of a future show champion should have excellent qualifications themselves.

The gender of your puppy is largely a matter of personal taste, and coloration is not a grave concern with this breed, but you may expect to pay more for harlequins and blacks. Fawns seem to be the most popular and most common. Nevertheless, a good stable dog with a great temperament can be any color, so poten-

Seeing the dam helps you predict how your puppy will mature; watching the pup with his mother and littermates tells volumes about his personality.

tial owners should not limit their selection to only one color unless they really have their hearts set on a particular color.

Always check the bite of your selected puppy to be sure that it is neither overshot nor undershot; minor faults may correct themselves as the dog grows, but major ones will not and may worsen.

Because litters are large and because Great Danes are very popular as pets, commercial breeders are attracted to the breed. Therefore, be careful when selecting your breeder and pup, ensuring that your chosen pup comes from a good line unencumbered by overbreeding, inbreeding or the countless finicky prejudices that have damaged other breeds. A breeder will commonly allow visitors to see the litter by around the fifth or sixth week, and puppies leave for their new homes between the eighth and tenth week. Breeders who permit their puppies to leave early are

> ### ARE YOU PREPARED?
> Unfortunately, when a puppy is bought by someone who does not take into consideration the time and attention that dog ownership requires, it is the puppy who suffers when he is either abandoned or placed in a shelter by a frustrated owner. So all of the "homework" you do in preparation for your pup's arrival will benefit you both. The more informed you are, the more you will know what to expect and the better equipped you will be to handle the ups and downs of raising a puppy. Hopefully, everyone in the household is willing to do his part in raising and caring for the pup. The anticipation of owning a dog often brings a lot of promises from excited family members: "I will walk him every day," "I will feed him," "I will housebreak him," etc., but these things take time and effort, and promises can easily be forgotten once the novelty of the new pet has worn off.

The pup should be curious and eager to meet you—this pup steps up to say hello to whoever's on the other side of the fence.

more interested in making a profit than in their puppies' well-being. Puppies need to learn the rules of the trade from their dams, and most dams continue teaching the pups manners and dos and don'ts until around the eighth week. Breeders spend significant amounts of time with the Great Dane toddlers during this time so that they are able to interact with the "other species," i.e., humans. Given the long history that dogs and humans have, bonding between the two species is natural but must be nurtured. A well-bred, well-socialized Great Dane pup wants nothing more than to be near you and please you.

COMMITMENT OF OWNERSHIP

After considering all of these factors, you have most likely already made some very important decisions about selecting your puppy. You have chosen the Great Dane, which means that you have decided which characteristics you want in a dog and what type of dog will best fit into your family and lifestyle. If you have selected a breeder, you have gone a step further—you have done your research and found a responsible, conscientious person who breeds quality Great Danes and who should be a reliable source of help as you and your puppy adjust to life together. If you have observed a litter in action, you have obtained a firsthand look at the dynamics of a puppy "pack" and, thus, you should have learned about each pup's individual personality—perhaps you have even found one that particularly appeals to you.

However, even if you have not yet found the Great Dane puppy of your dreams, observing pups will help you learn to recognize certain behavior and to determine what a pup's behavior indicates about his temperament. You will be able to pick out which pups are the leaders, which ones are less outgoing, which ones are confident, which ones are shy, playful, friendly, aggressive, etc. Equally as important, you will learn to recognize what a healthy pup should look and act like. All of these things will help you in your search, and when you find the Great Dane that was meant for you, you will know it!

Researching your breed, selecting a responsible breeder and observing as many pups as

TIME TO GO HOME

Breeders rarely release puppies until they are eight to ten weeks of age. This is an acceptable age for most breeds of dog, excepting toy breeds, which are not released until around 12 weeks, given their petite sizes. If a breeder has a puppy that is 12 weeks of age or older, it is likely well socialized and housebroken. Be sure that the puppy is otherwise healthy before deciding to take him home.

Pups that do as much growing as the Great Dane need a lot of rest! If the litter is napping when you visit, make a second trip to see the pups in action.

possible are all important steps on the way to dog ownership. It may seem like a lot of effort...and you have not even taken the pup home yet! Remember, though, you cannot be too careful when it comes to deciding on the type of dog you want and finding out about your prospective pup's background. Buying a puppy is not—or *should* not be—just another whimsical purchase. This is one instance in which you actually do get to choose your own family! You may be thinking that buying a puppy should be fun—it should not be so serious and so much work. Keep in mind that your puppy is not a cuddly stuffed toy or decorative lawn ornament, but a creature that will become a real member of your family. You will come to realize that, while buying a puppy is a pleasurable and exciting endeavor, it is not something to be taken lightly. Relax...the fun will start when the pup comes home!

Always keep in mind that a puppy is nothing more than a baby in a furry disguise...a baby who is virtually helpless in a human world and who trusts his owner for fulfillment of his basic needs for survival. In addition to food, water and shelter, your pup needs care, protection, guidance and love. If you are not prepared to commit to this, then you are not prepared to own a dog.

ARE YOU A FIT OWNER?

If the breeder from whom you are buying a puppy asks you a lot of personal questions, do not be insulted. Such a breeder wants to be sure that you will be a fit provider for his puppy.

"Wait a minute," you say. "How hard could this be? All of my neighbors own dogs and they seem to be doing just fine. Why should I have to worry about all of this?" Well, you should not worry about it; in fact, you will probably find that once your Great Dane pup gets used to his new home, he will fall into his place in the family quite naturally. But it never hurts to emphasize the commitment of dog ownership. With some time and patience, it is really not too difficult to raise a curious and exuberant Great Dane pup to be a well-adjusted and well-mannered adult dog—a dog that could be your most loyal friend.

PREPARING PUPPY'S PLACE IN YOUR HOME

Researching your breed and finding a breeder are only two aspects of the "homework" you will have to do before bringing your Great Dane puppy home. You will also have to prepare your home and family for the new addition. Much as you would prepare a nursery for a newborn baby, you will need to designate a place in your home that will be the puppy's own. How you prepare your home will depend on how much freedom the dog will be allowed. Whatever you decide, you must ensure that he has a place that he can "call his own."

When you bring your new puppy into your home, you are

"YOU BETTER SHOP AROUND!"

Finding a reputable breeder that sells healthy pups is very important, but make sure that the breeder you choose is not only someone you respect but also someone with whom you feel comfortable. Your breeder will be a resource long after you buy your puppy, and you must be able to call with reasonable questions without being made to feel like a pest! If you don't connect on a personal level, investigate some other breeders before making a final decision.

bringing him into what will become his home as well. Obviously, you did not buy a puppy so that he could take control of your house, but in order for a puppy to grow into a stable, well-adjusted dog, he has to feel comfortable in his surroundings. Remember, he is leaving the warmth and security of his mother and littermates, as well as the familiarity of the only place he has ever known, so it is important to make his transition as easy as possible. By preparing a place in your home for the puppy, you are making him feel as welcome as possible in a strange new place. It should not take him long to get used to it, but the sudden shock of being transplanted is somewhat traumatic for a young pup. Imagine how a small child would feel in the same situation—that is how your puppy

INHERIT THE MIND
In order to know whether or not a puppy will fit into your lifestyle, you need to assess his personality. A good way to do this is to interact with his parents. Your pup inherits not only his appearance but also his personality and temperament from the sire and dam. If the parents are fearful or overly aggressive, these same traits may show up in your puppy.

must be feeling. It is up to you to reassure him and to let him know, "Little guy, you are going to like it here!"

WHAT YOU SHOULD BUY

CRATE
To someone unfamiliar with the use of crates in dog training, it

To a curious pup, your home is uncharted territory that needs to be explored! You will have to prepare your home and set boundaries for your pup so that his "expeditions" won't cause him harm.

may seem like punishment to shut a dog in a crate, but this is not the case at all. More and more breeders and trainers are recommending crates as preferred tools for pet puppies as well as show puppies. Crates are not cruel—crates have many humane and highly effective uses in dog care and training. For example, crate-training is a very popular and very successful housebreaking method, a crate can keep your dog safe during travel and, perhaps most importantly, a crate provides your dog with a place of his own in your home. It serves as a "doggie bedroom" of sorts—your Great Dane can curl up in his crate when he wants to sleep or when he just needs a break. Many dogs sleep in their crates overnight. When lined with soft bedding and with a favorite toy inside, a crate becomes a cozy pseudo-den for your dog. Like his ancestors, he too will seek out the comfort and retreat of a den—you just happen to be providing him with something a little more luxurious than what his early ancestors enjoyed.

As far as purchasing a crate, the type that you buy is up to you. It will most likely be one of the two most popular types: wire or fiberglass. There are advantages and disadvantages to each type. For example, a wire crate is recommended for use in the home as it is more open, allowing the air to flow

QUALITY FOOD
The Great Dane's food must be mentioned. All dogs need a good-quality food with an adequate supply of protein to develop their bones and muscles properly, and this is especially essential with giant breeds, as the pups do much more growing than average-size dogs. Take the advice of your breeder, who can guide you in feeding your puppy and eventually switching to an adult diet.

through and affording the dog a view of what is going on around him. A fiberglass crate is sturdier and can double as a travel crate, providing protection for the dog.

The size of the crate is another thing to consider. Puppies do not stay puppies forever—in fact, sometimes it seems as if Great Dane pups grow right before your eyes. Unless you have the money and the inclination to buy a new crate every time your pup

PHOTO COURTESY OF DOSKOCIL.

blanket, will help the dog feel more at home. These things will take the place of the leaves, twigs, etc., that the pup would use in the wild to make a den; the pup can make his own "burrow" in the crate. Although your pup is far removed from his den-making ancestors, the denning instinct is still a part of his genetic makeup. Also, until you bring your pup home, he has been sleeping amid the warmth of his mother and littermates, and while a blanket is not the same as a warm, breathing body, it still provides heat and something with which to snuggle.

Your local pet shop should have a selection of crates, but be certain to obtain a giant-sized crate to accommodate your Great Dane.

has a growth spurt, it is better to get one that will accommodate your dog both as a pup and at full size. An extra-large crate will be necessary for a full-grown Great Dane, who stands upwards of 28 inches high at the shoulder.

BEDDING
Bedding in the dog's crate, such as a nice soft crate pad and a cuddly

---

CRATE-TRAINING TIPS
During crate training, you should partition off the section of the crate in which the pup stays. If he is given too big an area, this will hinder your training efforts. Crate training is based on the fact that a dog does not like to soil his sleeping quarters, so it is ineffective to keep a pup in an area that is so big that he can eliminate in one end and get far enough away from it to sleep. Also, you want to make the crate den-like for the pup. Blankets and a favorite toy will make the crate cozy for the small pup; as he grows, you may want to evict some of his "roommates" to make more room. It will take some coaxing at first, but be patient. Given some time to get used to it, your pup will adapt to his new home-within-a-home quite nicely.

Apart from the aforementioned reasons, soft bedding is very important in preventing the Great Dane from developing calluses on his elbows due to the weight put on them when the dog is lying down. You will want to wash your pup's bedding frequently in case he has an accident in his crate, and replace or remove anything that becomes ragged and starts to fall apart.

Toys

Toys are a must for dogs of all ages, especially for curious playful pups. Puppies are the "children" of the dog world, and what child does not love toys? Chew toys provide enjoyment to both dog and owner—your dog will enjoy playing with his favorite toys, while you will enjoy the fact that they distract him from your expensive shoes and leather couch. Puppies love to chew; in fact, chewing is a physical need for pups as they are teething, and everything looks appetizing! The full range of your possessions—from old dish rag to Oriental carpet—are fair game in the eyes of a teething pup. Puppies are not all that discerning when it comes to finding something to literally "sink their teeth into"—everything tastes great!

Great Dane puppies are fairly aggressive chewers and only the strongest toys should be offered to them. Breeders advise owners to

TOYS, TOYS, TOYS!
With a big variety of dog toys available, and so many that look like they would be a lot of fun for a dog, be careful in your selection. It is amazing what a set of puppy teeth can do to an innocent-looking toy; so, obviously, safety is a major consideration. Be sure to choose the most durable products that you can find. Hard nylon bones and toys are a safe bet, and many of them are offered in different scents and flavors that will be sure to capture your dog's attention. It is always fun to play a game of fetch with your dog, and there are balls and flying discs that are specially made to withstand dog teeth.

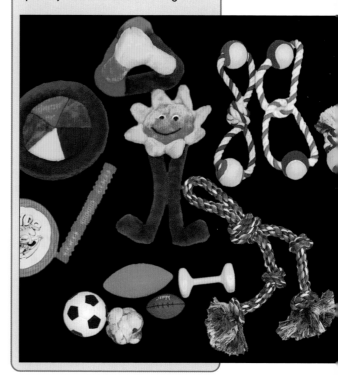

PLAY'S THE THING

Teaching the puppy to play with his toys in running and fetching games is an ideal way to help the puppy develop muscle, learn motor skills and bond with you, his owner and master. He also needs to learn how to inhibit his bite reflex and never to use his teeth on people, forbidden objects and other animals in play. Whenever you play with your puppy, you make the rules. Even in play, you must encourage your dog to behave—never allow him to be possessive with his toys or to act in a hyper manner. This becomes an important message to your puppy in teaching him that you are the pack leader and control everything he does in life. Once your dog accepts you as his leader, your relationship with him will be cemented for life.

resist stuffed toys, because they can become de-stuffed in no time. The overly excited pup may ingest the stuffing, which is neither nutritious nor digestible. Soft toys will be welcomed during teething, but only under your supervision.

Similarly, squeaky toys are quite popular, but must be avoided for the Great Dane. Perhaps a squeaky toy can be used as an aid in training, but not for free play. If a pup "disembowels" one of these, the small plastic squeaker inside can be dangerous if swallowed.

Be careful of natural bones, which have a tendency to splinter into sharp, dangerous pieces. Also be careful of rawhide, which can turn into pieces that are easy to swallow or into a mushy mess on your carpet. Monitor the condition of all your pup's toys carefully and get rid of any that have been chewed to the point of becoming potentially dangerous.

Leash

A nylon leash is probably the best option, as it is the most resistant to puppy teeth should your pup take a liking to chewing on his leash. Of course, this is a habit that should be nipped in the bud, but, if your pup likes to chew on his leash, he has a very slim chance of being able to chew through the strong nylon. Nylon leashes are also lightweight, which is good for a young Great

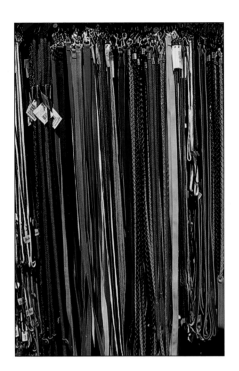

leash to something! A lightweight nylon collar is a good choice; make sure that it fits snugly enough so that the pup cannot wriggle out of it, but is loose enough so that it will not be uncomfortably tight around the pup's neck. You should be able to fit a finger between the pup and the collar. It may take some time for your pup to get used to wearing the collar, but soon he will not even notice that it is there. Again, with the adult Great Dane, you'll need a stronger collar. Choke collars are made for training, but should only be used by owners who have been instructed in their proper use.

FOOD AND WATER BOWLS

Your pup will need two bowls, one for food and one for water. You may want two sets of bowls,

Your local pet shop will have a large variety of leashes from which you can choose a sturdy leash for your Great Dane.

Dane who is just getting used to the idea of walking on a leash. For everyday walking and safety purposes, the nylon leash is a good choice.

As your pup grows up, and gets bigger and stronger, you will need to purchase a stronger leash, such as one made of thick leather. Of course there are special leashes for training purposes, but these are neither necessary nor recommended for routine walks.

COLLAR

Your pup should get used to wearing a collar all the time since you will want to attach his ID tags to it. Plus, you have to attach the

FINANCIAL RESPONSIBILITY
Grooming tools, collars, leashes, a crate, a dog bed and, of course, toys will be expenses to you when you first obtain your pup, and the cost will continue throughout your dog's lifetime. If your puppy damages or destroys your possessions (as most puppies surely will!) or something belonging to a neighbor, you can calculate additional expense. There is also flea and pest control, which every dog owner faces more than once. You must be able to handle the financial responsibility of owning a dog.

CHOOSE AN APPROPRIATE COLLAR

The **BUCKLE COLLAR** is the standard collar used for everyday purposes. Be sure that you adjust the buckle on growing puppies. Check it every day. It can become too tight overnight! These collars can be made of leather or nylon. Attach your dog's identification tags to this collar.

The **CHOKE COLLAR** is the designed for training. It is constructed of highly polished steel so that it slides easily through the stainless steel loop. The idea is that the dog controls the pressure around his neck and he will stop pulling if the collar becomes uncomfortable. *Never* leave a choke collar on your dog when not training.

The **HALTER** is for a trained dog that has to be restrained to prevent running away, chasing a cat and the like. Considered the most humane of all collars, it is frequently used on smaller dogs on which collars are not comfortable.

one for inside and one for outside, depending on where the dog will be fed and where he will be spending most of his time. Stainless steel or sturdy plastic bowls are popular choices. Plastic bowls are more chewable. Dogs tend not to chew on the steel variety, which can be sterilized. It is important to buy sturdy bowls since anything is in danger of being chewed by puppy teeth and you do not want your dog to be constantly chewing apart his bowl (for his safety and for your wallet!). Make sure the bowls are of adequate size, and purchase stands on which to elevate them.

CLEANING SUPPLIES

Until a pup is housebroken, you will be doing a lot of cleaning. "Accidents" will occur, which is okay in the beginning because the puppy does not know any better. All you can do is be prepared to clean up any accidents. Old rags, paper towels, newspapers and a safe disinfectant are good to have on hand.

BEYOND THE BASICS

The items previously discussed are the bare necessities. You will find out what else you need as you go along—grooming supplies, flea/tick protection, baby gates to partition a room, etc. These things will vary depending on your situation, but it is important that you have everything you need to feed

You will need large, sturdy food and water bowls for your Great Dane. Stands for the bowls are a necessity; eating and drinking from elevated bowls reduces the Great Dane's need to crane his neck, and thus reduces the risk of his swallowing air and developing bloat.

PHOTO COURTESY OF MIKKI PET PRODUCTS.

The rapidly growing Great Dane pup will soon be able to get into things that were previously out of reach. Keep this in mind when providing a puppy-proof environment indoors and out.

and make your Great Dane comfortable in his first few days at home.

PUPPY-PROOFING YOUR HOME

Aside from making sure that your Great Dane will be comfortable in your home, you also have to make sure that your home is safe for your Great Dane. This means taking precautions that your pup will not get into anything he should not get into and that there is nothing within his reach that may harm him should he sniff it, chew it, inspect it, etc. This probably seems obvious since, while

you are primarily concerned with your pup's safety, at the same time you do not want your belongings to be ruined. Breakables should be placed out of reach if your dog is to have full run of the house. If he is to be limited to certain places within the house, keep any potentially dangerous items in the "off-limits" areas. An electrical cord can pose a danger should the puppy decide to taste it—and who is going to convince a pup that it would not make a great chew toy? Cords should be kept from puppy teeth and fastened tightly against the wall. If your dog is going to spend time in a crate, make sure that there is nothing near his crate that he can reach if he sticks his curious little nose or paws through the openings. Just as you would with a

PET INSURANCE

Just like you can insure your car, your house and your own health, you likewise can insure your dog's health. Investigate a pet insurance policy by talking to your vet. Depending on the age of your dog, the breed and the kind of coverage you desire, your policy can be very affordable. Most policies cover accidental injuries, poisoning, and thousands of medical problems and illnesses, including cancers. Some carriers also offer routine care and immunization coverage.

child, keep all household cleaners and chemicals where the pup cannot get to them.

It is also important to make sure that the outside of your home is safe. Of course, your puppy should never be unsupervised, but a pup let loose in the yard will want to run and explore, and he should be granted that freedom. Do not let a fence give you a false sense of security; you would be surprised how crafty (and persistent) a dog can be in working out how to dig under and squeeze his way through holes, or to jump or climb over a fence. The remedy is to make the fence high enough so that it really is impossible for your dog to get over it (at least 6 feet should suffice), and well embedded into the ground. Be sure to repair or secure any gaps in the fence. Check the fence periodically to ensure that it is in good shape and make repairs as needed; a very determined pup may return to the same spot to "work on it" until he is able to get through.

FIRST TRIP TO THE VET

You have picked out your puppy, and your home and family are ready. Now all you have to do is collect your Great Dane from the breeder and the fun begins, right? Well...not so fast. Something else you need to prepare is your pup's first trip to the veterinarian. Perhaps the breeder can recommend someone in the area who

specializes in Great Danes or giant-breed dogs, or maybe you know some other Great Dane owners who can suggest a good vet. Either way, you should have

NATURAL TOXINS

Examine your lawn and home landscaping before bringing your puppy home. Many varieties of plants have leaves, stems or flowers that are toxic if ingested, and you can depend on a curious puppy to investigate them. Ask your vet for information on poisonous plants or research them at your library.

an appointment arranged for your pup before you pick him up and plan on taking him for an examination before bringing him home.

The pup's first visit will consist of an overall examination to make sure that he does not have any problems that are not apparent to you. The veterinarian will also set up a schedule for the pup's vaccinations; the breeder will inform you of which ones the pup has already received and the vet can continue from there.

TOXIC PLANTS

Many plants can be toxic to dogs. If you see your dog carrying a piece of vegetation in his mouth, approach him in a quiet, disinterested manner, avoid eye contact, pet him and gradually remove the plant from his mouth. Alternatively, offer him a treat and maybe he'll drop the plant on his own accord. Be sure no toxic plants are growing in your own home or garden.

INTRODUCTION TO THE FAMILY

Everyone in the house will be excited about the puppy's coming home and will want to pet him and play with him, but it is best to make the introduction low-key so as not to overwhelm the puppy. He is apprehensive already. It is the first time he has been separated from his mother and the breeder, and the ride to your home is likely to be the first time he has been in a car. The last thing you want to do is smother him, as this will only frighten him further. This is not to say that human contact is not extremely necessary at this stage, because this is the time when a connection between the pup and his human family is formed. Gentle petting and soothing words should help console him, as well as just putting him down and letting him explore on his own (under your watchful eye, of course).

The pup may approach the family members or may busy himself with exploring for a while. Gradually, each person should spend some time with the pup, one at a time, crouching down to get as close to the pup's level as possible, letting the pup sniff his hands and petting the pup gently. The puppy definitely needs human attention and needs to be touched—this is how to form an immediate bond. Just remember that the pup is experiencing a

SKULL & CROSSBONES

Thoroughly puppy-proof your house before bringing your puppy home. Never use cockroach or rodent poisons or plant fertilizers in any area accessible to the puppy. Avoid the use of toilet cleaners. Most dogs are born with "toilet-bowl sonar" and will take a drink if the lid is left open. Also keep the trash secured and out of reach. Scour your garage for potential puppy dangers. Remove weed killers, pesticides and antifreeze materials. Antifreeze is highly toxic and just a few drops can kill a puppy or an adult dog. The sweet taste attracts the animal, who will quickly consume it from the floor or pavement.

lot of things for the first time, at the same time. There are new people, new noises, new smells and new things to investigate, so be gentle, be affectionate and be as comforting as you can be.

PUP'S FIRST NIGHT HOME

You have traveled home with your new charge safely in his crate. He's been to the vet for a thorough check-up; he's been weighed, his papers examined; perhaps he's even been vaccinated and wormed as well. He's met the family and licked the whole family, including the excited children and the less-than-happy cat. He's explored his area, his new bed, the yard and anywhere else he's been permitted. He's eaten

his first meal at home and relieved himself in the proper place. He's heard lots of new sounds, smelled new friends and seen more of the outside world than ever before.

That was just the first day! He's worn out and is ready for bed...or so you think! It's puppy's first night and you are ready to say "Good night"—keep in mind that this is puppy's first night ever to be sleeping alone. His dam and littermates are no longer at paw's length and he's a bit scared, cold and lonely. Be reassuring to your new family member, but this is not the time to spoil him and give in to his inevitable whining.

Puppies whine. They whine to let others know where they are and hopefully to get company out of it. Place your pup in his new bed or crate in his room and close the crate door. Mercifully, he may fall asleep without a peep. When the inevitable occurs, ignore the

Have an array of safe toys ready for your puppy's arrival and spend some playtime with him to help him settle in.

whining; he is fine. Be strong and keep his interest in mind. Do not allow your heart to become guilty and visit the pup. He will fall asleep.

MANNERS MATTER

During the socialization process, a puppy should meet people, experience different environments and definitely be exposed to other canines. Through playing and interacting with other dogs, your puppy will learn lessons, ranging from controlling the pressure of his jaws by biting his littermates to the inner-workings of the canine pack that he will apply to his human relationships for the rest of his life. That is why removing a puppy from his litter too early (before eight weeks) can be detrimental to the pup's development.

Many breeders recommend placing a piece of bedding from his former home in his new bed so that he recognizes the scent of his littermates. Others still advise placing a hot water bottle in his bed for warmth. This latter may be a good idea provided the pup doesn't attempt to suckle—he'll get good and wet and may not fall asleep so fast.

Puppy's first night can be somewhat stressful for the pup and his new family. Remember that you are setting the tone of nighttime at your house. Unless you want to play with your pup every night at 10 p.m., midnight and 2 a.m., don't initiate the habit. Your family will thank you, and eventually so will your pup!

PREVENTING PUPPY PROBLEMS

SOCIALIZATION

Now that you have done all of the preparatory work and have helped your pup get accustomed to his new home and family, it is about time for you to have some fun! Socializing your Great Dane pup gives you the opportunity to show off your new friend, and your pup gets to reap the benefits of being an adorable gangly creature that people will want to pet and, in general, think is absolutely precious!

Besides getting to know his new family, your puppy should be exposed to other people, animals and situations, but of course he must not come into close contact with dogs you don't know well until his course of injections is fully complete. Socialization will help him become well adjusted as he grows up and less prone to being timid or fearful of the new things he will encounter. Your pup's socialization began at the breeder's, but now it is your responsibility to continue it. The socialization he receives up until the age of 12 weeks is the most critical, as this is the time when he forms his impressions of the outside world. Be especially careful during the eight-to-ten-week-old period, also known as the fear period. The interaction he receives during this time should be gentle and reassuring. Lack of socialization can manifest itself in fear and aggression as the dog grows up. He needs lots of human contact, affection, handling and exposure to other animals.

Once your pup has received his necessary vaccinations, feel free to take him out and about (on his leash, of course). Walk him around the neighborhood, take him on your daily errands, let people pet him, let him meet other dogs and pets, etc. Puppies do not have to try to make friends; there will be no shortage of people who will want to introduce themselves. Just make sure that you carefully supervise each

PROPER SOCIALIZATION

The socialization period for puppies is from age 8 to 16 weeks. This is the time when puppies need to leave their birth family and take up residence with their new owners, where they will meet many new people, other pets, etc. Failure to be adequately socialized can cause the dog to grow up fearing others and being shy and unfriendly due to a lack of self-confidence.

meeting. If the neighborhood children want to say hello, for example, that is great—children and pups most often make great companions. However, sometimes an excited child can unintentionally handle a pup too roughly, or an overzealous pup can playfully nip a little too hard. You want to make socialization experiences positive ones. What a pup learns during this very formative stage will impact his attitude toward future encounters. You want your

DOG MEETS WORLD
Thorough socialization includes not only meeting new people but also being introduced to new experiences such as riding in the car, having his coat brushed, hearing the television, walking in a crowd—the list is endless. The more your Great Dane experiences as a pup, and the more positive the experiences are, the less of a shock and the less frightening it will be for your dog to encounter new things.

dog to be comfortable around everyone. A pup that has a bad experience with a child may grow up to be a dog that is shy around or aggressive toward children.

CONSISTENCY IN TRAINING
Dogs, being pack animals, naturally need a leader, or else they try to establish dominance in their packs. When you bring a dog into your family, the choice of who becomes the leader and who becomes the "pack" is entirely up to you! Your pup's intuitive quest for dominance, coupled with the fact that it is nearly impossible to look at an adorable Great Dane pup, with his "puppy-dog" eyes and feet he hasn't quite yet grown into, and not cave in, give the pup almost an unfair advantage in getting the upper hand!

A pup will definitely test the waters to see what he can and cannot do. Do not give in to those pleading eyes—stand your ground when it comes to disciplining the pup and make sure that all family members do the same. It will only confuse the pup when Mother tells him to get off the couch when he is used to sitting up there with Father to watch the nightly news. Avoid discrepancies by having all members of the household decide on the rules before the pup even comes home…and be consistent in enforcing them! Early training shapes the dog's personality, so you cannot be unclear in what you expect.

COMMON PUPPY PROBLEMS
The best way to prevent puppy problems is to be proactive in stopping an undesirable behavior as soon as it starts. The old saying "You can't teach an old dog new tricks" does not necessarily hold true, but it *is* true that it is much easier to discourage bad behavior in a young developing pup than to wait until the pup's bad behavior becomes the adult dog's bad habit. There are some problems that are

CHEWING TIPS

Chewing goes hand in hand with nipping in the sense that a teething puppy is always looking for a way to soothe his aching gums. In this case, instead of chewing on you, he may have taken a liking to your favorite shoe or something else that he should not be chewing. Again, realize that this is a normal canine behavior that does not need to be discouraged, only redirected. Your pup just needs to be taught what is acceptable to chew on and what is off-limits. Consistently tell him "No!" when you catch him chewing on something forbidden and give him a chew toy.

Conversely, praise him when you catch the puppy chewing on something appropriate. In this way, you are discouraging the inappropriate behavior and reinforcing the desired behavior. The puppy's chewing should stop after his adult teeth have come in, but an adult dog continues to chew for various reasons—perhaps because he is bored, needs to relieve tension or just likes to chew. That is why it is important to redirect his chewing when he is still young.

especially prevalent in puppies as they develop.

NIPPING

As puppies start to teethe, they feel the need to sink their teeth into anything available...unfortunately that includes your fingers, arms, hair and toes. You may find this behavior cute for the first five seconds...until you feel just how sharp those puppy teeth are. This is something you want to discourage immediately and consistently with a firm "No!" (or whatever number of firm "Nos" it takes for him to understand that you mean business). Then replace your finger with an appropriate chew toy. While this behavior is merely annoying when the dog is young, it can become dangerous as your Great Dane's adult teeth grow in and his jaws develop, and he continues to think it is okay to gnaw on human appendages. Your Great Dane does not mean any harm with a friendly nip, but he also does not know his own strength.

CRYING/WHINING

Your pup will often cry, whine, whimper, howl or make some type of commotion when he is left alone. This is basically his way of calling out for attention to make sure that you know he is there and that you have not forgotten about him. He feels insecure when he is left alone, when you are out of the house and he is in his crate or when you are in another part of the house and he cannot see you. The noise he is making is an expression of the anxiety he feels at being alone, so he needs to be taught that being alone is okay. You are not actually training the dog to stop making noise, you are training him to feel comfortable when he is alone and thus removing the need for him to make the noise.

This is where the crate with cozy bedding and a toy comes in handy. You want to know that he is safe when you are not there to supervise, and you know that he will be safe in his crate rather than roaming freely about the house. In order for the pup to stay in his crate without making a fuss, he needs to be comfortable in his crate. On that note, it is extremely important that the crate is never used as a form of punishment, or the pup will have a negative association with the crate.

Accustom the pup to the crate in short, gradually increasing time intervals in which you put him in the crate, maybe with a treat, and stay in the room with him. If he cries or makes a fuss, do not go to him, but stay in his sight. Gradually he will realize that staying in his crate is okay without your help, and it will not be so traumatic for him when you are not around. You may want to leave the radio on softly when you leave the house; the sound of human voices may be comforting to him.

NO CHOCOLATE!

Use treats to bribe your dog into a desired behavior. Try small pieces of hard cheese or freeze-dried liver. *Never* offer chocolate, as it has toxic qualities for dogs.

DIETARY AND FEEDING CONSIDERATIONS

Today the choices of food for your Great Dane are many and varied. There are simply dozens of brands of food in all sorts of flavors and textures, ranging from puppy diets to those for seniors. There are even hypoallergenic and low-calorie diets available. Because your Great Dane's food has a bearing on coat, health and temperament, it is essential that the most suitable diet be selected for a Great Dane of his age. It is fair to say, however, that even dedicated owners can be some-what perplexed by the enormous range of foods available. Only understanding what is best for your dog will help you reach an informed decision.

Dog foods are produced in three basic types: dry, semi-moist and canned. Dry foods are useful for the cost-conscious, for overall they tend to be less expensive than semi-moist or canned. These contain the least fat and the most preservatives. In general, canned foods are made up of 60–70% water, while semi-moist ones often contain so much sugar that they

FEEDING TIPS

Dog food must be served at room temperature, neither too hot nor too cold. Fresh water, changed often and offered in a clean bowl, is mandatory, especially when feeding dry food.

Never feed your dog from the table while you are eating, and never feed your dog leftovers from your own meal. They usually contain too much fat and too much seasoning.

Dogs must chew their food. Hard pellets are excellent; soups and stews are to be avoided. Don't add any extras to commercial dog food, as it is usually balanced, and adding something extra destroys the balance. Supplementation should *only* be advised by the vet or breeder.

Except for age-related changes, dogs do not require dietary variations. They can be fed the same diet, day after day, without becoming bored or ill.

are perhaps the least preferred by owners, even though their dogs seem to like them.

When selecting your dog's diet, three stages of development must be considered: the puppy stage, adult stage and senior stage.

PUPPY STAGE

Puppies instinctively want to suck milk from their mother's teats and a normal puppy will exhibit this behavior from just a few moments following birth. If puppies do not attempt to suckle within the first half-hour or so, the breeder should encourage them to do so by placing them on the nipples, having selected ones with plenty of milk. This early milk supply is important in providing colostrum to protect the puppies during the first eight to ten weeks of their lives. Although a mother's milk is much better than any milk formula, despite there being some excellent ones available, if the puppies do not feed, the breeder will have to feed them himself. For those with less experience, advice from a veterinarian is important so that not only the right quantity of milk is fed but also that of correct quality, fed at suitably frequent intervals, usually every two hours during the first few days of life.

Puppies should be allowed to nurse from their mothers for about the first six weeks, although from the third or fourth week the breeder will begin to introduce

The best food for puppies during their first weeks of life is their mother's milk.

Don't make your dog reach down for his food—and it's a long reach for the Great Dane! Elevated bowls aid digestion and prevent bloat.

small portions of suitable solid food. Most breeders like to introduce alternate milk and meat meals initially, building up to weaning time.

Great Dane pups should be fed three meals per day when they are six to eight weeks of age. At eight weeks, the pup can be fed twice per day. Fussy eaters may require an additional smaller meal to maintain a good weight.

There are differing opinions among breeders as to how much protein a growing pup needs, so take the breeder's advice based on the foods with which he has had success. Puppy and junior diets should be well balanced for the needs of your dog, so that except in certain circumstances additional vitamins, minerals and proteins will not be required.

CHANGE IN DIET

As your dog's caretaker, you know the importance of keeping his diet consistent, but sometimes when you run out of food or if you're on vacation, you have to make a change quickly. Some dogs will experience digestive problems, but most will not. If you are planning on changing your dog's menu, do so gradually to ensure that your dog will not have any problems. Over a period of four to five days, slowly add some new food to your dog's old food, increasing the percentage of new food each day.

Discuss your Great Dane puppy's diet with your breeder for the best advice about feeding his line of Great Danes. Some lines require more or less food than you might expect.

ADULT DIETS

A dog is considered an adult when he has stopped growing, so in general the diet of a Great Dane can be changed to an adult one at about 12 to 18 months of age. Again you should rely upon your vet or dietary specialist to recommend an acceptable maintenance diet. Major dog-food manufacturers specialize in this type of food, and it is just necessary for you to select the one best suited to your dog's needs. Active dogs may have different requirements than sedate dogs.

Great Danes don't need huge meals, like you may expect for their size, but some will certainly relish every last morsel!

> ### "DOES THIS COLLAR MAKE ME LOOK FAT?"
>
> While humans may obsess about how they look and how trim their bodies are, many people believe that extra weight on their dogs is a good thing. The truth is, pets should not be over- or underweight, as both can lead to or signal sickness. In order to tell how fit your pet is, run your hands over his ribs. Are his ribs buried under a layer of fat or are they sticking out considerably? If your pet is within his normal weight range, you should be able to feel the ribs easily, but they should not protrude abnormally. If you stand above him, the outline of his body should resemble an hourglass. Some breeds do tend to be leaner while some are a bit stockier, but making sure your dog is the right weight for his breed will certainly contribute to his good health.

A Great Dane is full grown by around 18 months of age, though it often takes another 12 to 18 months for dog to reach his peak as a performance animal.

SENIOR DIETS

As dogs get older, their metabolism changes. The older dog usually exercises less, moves more slowly and sleeps more. This change in lifestyle and physiological performance requires a change in diet. Since these changes take place slowly, they might not be recognizable.

Bring along some water on long walks or when you travel, and give your Great Dane frequent water breaks.

What is easily recognizable is weight gain. By continuing to feed your dog an adult-maintenance diet when he is slowing down metabolically, your dog will gain weight. Obesity in an older dog compounds the health problems that already accompany old age.

As your dog gets older, few of their organs function up to par. The kidneys slow down and the intestines become less efficient. These age-related factors are best handled with a change in diet and a change in feeding schedule to give smaller portions that are more easily digested.

There is no single best diet for every older dog. While many dogs do well on light or senior diets, other dogs do better on other special premium diets such as lamb and rice. Be sensitive to your senior Great Dane's diet and this will help control other problems that may arise with your old friend.

WATER

Just as your dog needs proper nutrition from his food, water is an essential "nutrient" as well. Water keeps the dog's body properly hydrated and promotes normal function of the body's systems. During housebreaking, it is necessary to keep an eye on how much water your Great Dane is drinking, but once he is reliably trained he should have

WALKING LIKE A PRO

For many people, it is difficult to imagine putting their dog's well-being in someone else's hands, but if you are unable to give your dog his necessary exercise breaks, hiring a professional dog walker may be a good idea. Dog walkers offer your dog exercise, a chance to work off energy and companionship—all things that keep your dog healthy. Seek referrals from your veterinarian, breeder or groomer to find a reputable dog walker.

access to clean fresh water at all times. Ensure that the dog's water bowl is clean and elevated on a bowl stand. Change the water often, making certain that water is always available for your dog, especially if you feed dry food.

EXERCISE

All dogs require some form of exercise, regardless of breed. A sedentary lifestyle is as harmful to a dog as it is to a person. The Great Dane happens to be an average breed when it comes to exercise requirements. Regular walks, play sessions in the yard or letting the dog run free in the fenced yard under your supervision are all sufficient forms of exercise for the Great Dane, once full grown. Exercise before the age of one year should be limited, as too much can damage the youngster's growing bones and cause skeletal prob-

lems. Pups also should not be allowed to climb stairs.

Bear in mind that an overweight dog should never be suddenly over-exercised; instead he should be allowed to increase exercise slowly. Remember that not only is exercise essential to keep the dog's body fit, it is essential to his mental well-being. A bored dog will find something to do, which often manifests itself in some type of destructive behavior. In this sense, it is essential for the owner's mental well-being as well!

GROOMING

BRUSHING

A natural bristle brush or a hound glove can be used for regular routine brushing. Daily brushing is effective for removing dirt and dead hair, and for stimulating the dog's natural oils to add shine and a healthy look to the coat. Although the Great Dane's coat is short and close, it does require a five-minute once-over to keep it looking its shiny best. Regular grooming sessions are also a good way to spend time with your dog. Many dogs grow to like the feel of being brushed and will enjoy the daily routine.

BATHING

Dogs do not need to be bathed as often as humans, but bathing as needed is important for clean skin

A metal grooming rake can be used to give the Great Dane's coat a once-over, combing in the direction in which the hair lies.

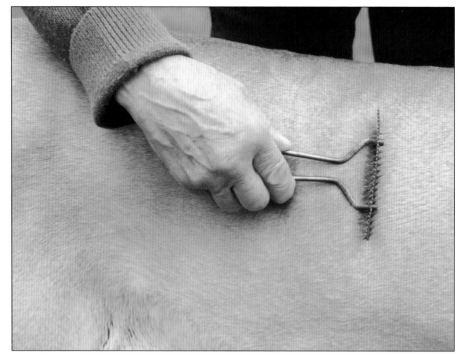

and a healthy, shiny coat. Again, like most anything, if you accustom your pup to being bathed as a puppy, it will be second nature by the time he grows up. You want your dog to be at ease during his bath or else it could end up a wet, soapy, messy ordeal for both of you!

Brush your Great Dane thoroughly before wetting his coat. This will get rid of loose hair and dirt in the coat. Make sure that your dog has a good non-slip surface to stand on. Begin by wetting the dog's coat. A shower or hose attachment is necessary for thoroughly wetting

and rinsing the dog. Depending on your living situation, you may opt to bathe your Dane outdoors on a mild day.

SOAP IT UP

The use of human soap products like shampoo, bubble bath and hand soap can be damaging to a dog's coat and skin. Human products are too strong; they remove the protective oils coating the dog's hair and skin that make him water-resistant. Use only shampoo made especially for dogs. You may like to use a medicated shampoo, which will help to keep external parasites at bay.

Next, apply shampoo to the dog's coat and work it into a good lather. You should purchase a shampoo that is made for dogs. Do not use a product made for human hair. Wash the head last; you do not want shampoo to drip into the dog's eyes while you are washing the rest of his body. Work the shampoo all the way down to the skin. You can use this opportunity to check the skin for any bumps, bites or other abnormalities. Do not neglect any area of the body—get all of the hard-to-reach places.

Once the dog has been thoroughly shampooed, he requires an equally thorough rinsing. Shampoo left in the coat can be irritating to the skin. Protect his eyes from the shampoo by shield-

A chamois cloth is used as a final step to leave the coat shiny.

ing them with your hand and directing the flow of water in the opposite direction. You should also avoid getting water in the ear canal. Be prepared for your dog to shake out his coat—you might want to stand back, but make sure you have a hold on the dog to keep him from getting away or getting into the grass or mud.

EAR CLEANING

The ears should be kept clean and any excess hair inside the ear should be carefully plucked out. Ears can be cleaned gently with a cotton ball and ear powder made especially for dogs; *never* enter the ear canal. Be on the lookout for any signs of infection or ear-mite infestation. If your Great Dane has been shaking his head or scratching at his ears frequently, this

---

BATHING BEAUTY

Once your dog is bathed, squeeze the excess water out of his coat with your hand and dry him with a heavy towel. You may choose to use a blow dryer set on the lowest setting on his coat or just let it dry naturally. In cold weather, never allow your dog outside with a wet coat.

There are "dry bath" products on the market, which are sprays and powders intended for spot cleaning, that can be used between regular baths if necessary. They are not substitutes for regular baths, but they are easy to use for touch-ups as they do not require rinsing.

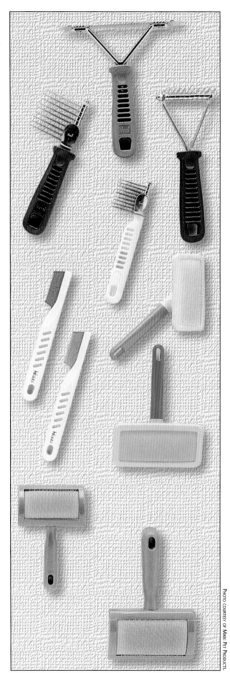

Your local pet shop will have a variety of grooming tools, brushes and combs that will assist you in keeping your Great Dane's coat in immaculate condition.

PHOTO COURTESY OF MIKKI PET PRODUCTS.

usually indicates a problem. If his ears have an unusual odor, this is a sure sign of mite infestation or infection, and a signal to have his ears checked by the veterinarian.

NAIL CLIPPING

Your Great Dane should be accustomed to having his nails trimmed at an early age, since it will be part of your maintenance routine throughout his life. Not only does it look nicer, but long nails can scratch someone unintentionally. Also, a long nail has a better chance of ripping and bleeding, or of causing the feet to spread. A good rule of thumb is that if you can hear your dog's nails' clicking on the floor when he walks, his nails are too long.

GROOMING EQUIPMENT

How much grooming equipment you purchase will depend on how much grooming you are going to do. Here are some basics:

- Natural bristle brush
- Grooming glove
- Flea comb
- Chamois
- Rubber mat
- Dog shampoo
- Spray hose attachment
- Towels
- Ear cleaner
- Cotton balls
- Nail clippers

Cropped ears are better ventilated than natural drop ears. Both types require care and gentle cleaning, never probing into the ear canal.

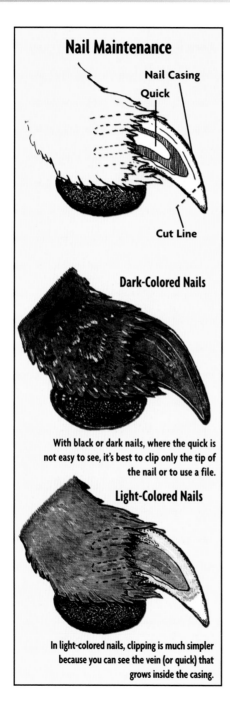

Nail Maintenance

Nail Casing

Quick

Cut Line

Dark-Colored Nails

With black or dark nails, where the quick is not easy to see, it's best to clip only the tip of the nail or to use a file.

Light-Colored Nails

In light-colored nails, clipping is much simpler because you can see the vein (or quick) that grows inside the casing.

Before you start cutting, make sure you can identify the "quick" in each nail. The quick is a blood vessel that runs through the center of each nail and grows rather close to the end. It will bleed if accidentally cut, which will be quite painful for the dog as it contains nerve endings. Keep some type of clotting agent on hand, such as a styptic pencil or styptic powder (the type used for shaving). This will stop the bleeding quickly when applied to the end of the cut nail. Do not panic if you cut the quick, just stop the bleeding and talk soothingly to your dog. Once he has calmed down, move on to the next nail. It is better to clip a little at a time, particularly with dark-nailed dogs.

Hold your pup steady as you begin trimming his nails; you do not want him to make any sudden movements or run away. Talk to him soothingly and stroke him as you clip. Holding his foot in your hand, simply take off the end of each nail in one quick clip. You can purchase nail clippers that are specially made for dogs; you can probably find them wherever you buy grooming supplies.

TRAVELING WITH YOUR DOG

CAR TRAVEL
You should accustom your Great Dane puppy to riding in a car at

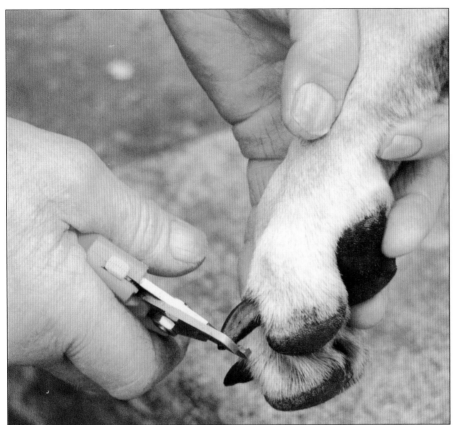

It is somewhat difficult to clip a Great Dane's nails because they are rather thick. You will need a strong pair of clippers and a careful hand to get the job done.

an early age. You may or may not take him in the car often, but at the very least he will need to go to the vet and you do not want these trips to be traumatic for the dog or problematic for you. The safest way for a dog to ride in the car is in his crate. If he uses a crate in the house, you can use the same crate for travel, providing your vehicle is large enough to accommodate a giant-sized crate.

Put the pup in the crate and see how he reacts. If he seems uneasy, you can have a passenger hold him on his lap while you drive. Of course, you will need to make other arrangements when your Great Dane is full grown! Another option is a specially made safety harness for dogs, which straps the dog in much like a seat belt. Owners with larger vehicles, like sport utility vehicles or station wagons, can partition the back of the vehicle to create a safe place for the dog. Do not let the dog roam loose in the vehicle—this is very dangerous! If you should stop short, your dog can be thrown and injured. If the dog starts climbing around you in the car, or pestering you while you are driving, you will not be able to concentrate on the road. It is an unsafe situation for everyone—human and canine.

Never leave your dog alone in the car. In hot weather, your dog can die from the high temperature inside a closed vehicle; even a car parked in the shade can heat up very quickly. Leaving the window open is dangerous as well since the dog can hurt himself trying to get out.

For long trips, be prepared to stop to let the dog relieve himself. Bring along whatever you need to clean up after him. You should

Although not the most portable of breeds, Great Danes enjoy doing things with their owners and will likely want to go with you when possible.

EXERCISE ALERT!
You should be careful where you exercise your dog. Many countryside areas have been sprayed with chemicals that are highly toxic to both dogs and humans. Never allow your dog to eat grass or drink from puddles on either public or private grounds, as the run-off water may contain chemicals from sprays and herbicides.

take along some paper towels and perhaps some old bath towels for use should he have an accident in the car or suffer from motion sickness.

AIR TRAVEL
Contact your chosen airline before proceeding with your travel plans that include your Great Dane. The dog will be required to travel in a fiberglass crate and you should always check in advance with the airline regarding specific requirements for the crate's size, type and

labeling; this is especially important with a giant-breed dog, as not all airlines will accept the oversized crates that are necessary to house a Great Dane.

If you are able to travel by air with your Dane, you'll want to make him as comfortable as possible. To help put the dog at ease, give him one of his favorite toys in the crate. Do not feed the dog for several hours prior to checking in so that you minimize his need to relieve himself. However, some airlines require that the dog must be fed within a certain time frame of arriving at the airport, in which case a light meal is best. For long trips, you will have to attach food and water bowls to the dog's crate so that airline employees can tend to him between legs of the trip.

Make sure that your dog is properly identified and that your contact information appears on his ID tags and on his crate. Your Great Dane will travel in a different area of the plane than the human passengers, so every rule must be strictly followed to prevent the risk of getting separated from your dog.

The need may arise for you to board your Great Dane, so be prepared by having a kennel selected ahead of time. Be sure the kennel is clean and large enough for your dog. Cost and convenience of location are two more factors to be considered.

VACATIONS AND BOARDING

So you want to take a family vacation—and you want to include *all* members of the family. You would probably make arrangements for accommodation ahead of time anyway, but this is especially important when traveling with a dog. You do not want to make an overnight stop at the only place around for miles and find out that they do not allow dogs. Also, you do not want to reserve a place for your family without confirming that you are traveling with a large dog because, if it is against their policy, you may end up without a place to stay.

Alternatively, if you are traveling and choose not to bring your Great Dane, you will have to make arrangements for him while you are away. Some options are to take him to a neighbor's house to stay while you are gone, to have a trusted neighbor stop in often or stay at your house or to bring your dog to a reputable boarding kennel. If you choose to board him at a kennel, you should visit in advance to see the facilities provided, how clean they are and where the dogs are kept. Talk to some of the employees and see how they treat the dogs—do they spend time with the dogs, play with them, exercise them, etc.? Also find out the kennel's policy on vaccinations and what they require. This is for all of the dogs' safety, since when dogs are kept together, there is a greater risk of diseases being passed from dog to dog.

IDENTIFICATION

Your Great Dane is your valued companion and friend. That is

IDENTIFICATION OPTIONS

As puppies become more and more expensive, especially those puppies of high quality for showing and/or breeding, they have a greater chance of being stolen. The usual collar dog tag is, of course, easily removed. But there are two more permanent techniques that have become widely used for identification.

The puppy microchip implantation involves the injection of a small microchip, about the size of a corn kernel, under the skin of the dog. If your dog shows up at a clinic or shelter, or is offered for resale under less-than-savory circumstances, it can be positively identified by the microchip. The microchip is scanned, and a registry quickly identifies you as the owner.

Tattooing is done on various parts of the dog, from his belly to his cheeks. The number tattooed can be your telephone number or any other number that you can easily memorize. When professional dog thieves see a tattooed dog, they usually lose interest. For the safety of our dogs, no laboratory facility or dog broker will accept a tattooed dog as stock. Both microchipping and tattooing can be done at your local veterinary clinic.

why you always keep a close eye on him and you have made sure that he cannot escape from the yard or wriggle out of his collar and run away from you. However, accidents can happen and there may come a time when your dog unexpectedly gets separated from you. If this unfortunate event should occur, the first thing on your mind will be finding him. Proper identification, including an ID tag and possibly a tattoo and/or microchip, will increase the chances of his being returned to you safely and quickly.

Tattoos have been the preferred method of identifying a dog for a number of years. The dog's thigh is a common place in which to put a tattoo; the area is shaved for the process. Microchips are also increasingly popular with dog owners. The chip, which is the size of a grain of uncooked rice, is implanted under the dog's loose skin over his shoulders. The chip (containing a unique number code) is readable by a scanner that emits low-frequency radio waves. The team responsible for the Home-Again microchip ID system, Schering-Plough Animal Health and Destry-Fearing, introduced a universal scanner capable of reading chips from all manufacturers. These scanners are set up in animal shelters around the country.

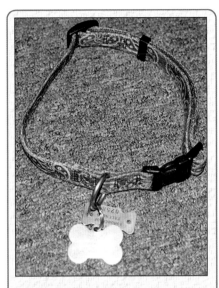

COLLAR REQUIRED

If your dog gets lost, he is not able to ask for directions home. Identification tags fastened to the collar give important information—the dog's name, the owner's name, the owner's address and a telephone number where the owner can be reached. This makes it easy for whoever finds the dog to contact the owner and arrange to have the dog returned. An added advantage is that a person will be more likely to approach a lost dog who has ID tags on his collar; it tells the person that this is somebody's pet rather than a stray. This is the easiest and fastest method of identification, provided that the tags stay on the collar and the collar stays on the dog.

If your dog was lost or stolen, you undoubtedly would become very upset. Likewise, if you encounter a lost dog, try to get in touch with the owners or notify the police or the local animal shelter.

TRAINING YOUR
GREAT DANE

REAP THE REWARDS

If you start with a normal, healthy dog and give him time, patience and some carefully executed lessons, you will reap the rewards of that training for the life of the dog. And what a life it will be! The two of you will find immeasurable pleasure in the companionship you have built together with love, respect and understanding.

Living with an untrained dog is a lot like owning a piano that you do not know how to play—it is a nice object to look at, but it does not do much more than that to bring you pleasure. Now try taking piano lessons, and suddenly the piano comes alive and brings forth magical sounds and rhythms that set your heart singing and your body swaying.

The same is true with your Great Dane. Any dog is a big responsibility and, if not trained sensibly, may develop unacceptable behavior that annoys you or could even cause family friction.

To train your Great Dane, you may like to enroll in an obedience class. Teach him good manners as you learn how and why he behaves the way he does. Find out how to communicate with your dog and how to recognize and understand his communications with you. Suddenly the dog takes on a new role in your life—he is clever, interesting, well-behaved and fun to be with. He demonstrates his bond of devotion to you daily. In other words, your Great Dane does wonders for your ego because he constantly reminds you that you are not only his leader, you are his hero!

THINK BEFORE YOU BARK

Dogs are sensitive to their masters' moods and emotions. Use your voice wisely when communicating with your dog. Never raise your voice at your dog unless you are trying to correct him. "Barking" at your dog can become as meaningless as "dogspeak" is to you.

Those involved with teaching dog obedience and counseling owners about their dogs' behavior have discovered some interesting facts about dog ownership. For example, training dogs when they are puppies results in the highest rate of success in developing well-mannered and well-adjusted adult dogs. Training an older dog, from six months to six years of age, can produce almost equal results, providing that the owner accepts the dog's slower rate of learning capability and is willing to work patiently to help the dog succeed at developing to his fullest potential. Unfortunately, many owners of untrained adult dogs lack the patience factor, so they do not persist until their dogs are successful at learning particular behaviors.

Training a puppy aged 10 to 16 weeks (20 weeks at the most) is like working with a dry sponge in a pool of water. The pup soaks up whatever you show him and constantly looks for more things to do and learn. At this early age,

A big part of training is setting boundaries for your dog and teaching him to observe them. This is how the dog becomes a well-behaved member of the family.

CALM DOWN

Dogs will do anything for your attention. If you reward the dog when he is calm and attentive, you will develop a well-mannered dog. If, on the other hand, you greet your dog excitedly and encourage him to jump up on you, the dog will greet you the same way and you will have a hyperactive dog on your hands.

his body is not yet producing hormones, and therein lies the reason for such a high rate of success. Without hormones, he is focused on his owner and not particularly interested in investigating other places, dogs, people, etc. You are his leader: his provider of food, water, shelter and security. He latches onto you and wants to stay close. He will usually follow you from room to room, will not let you out of his sight when you are outdoors with him and will respond in like manner to the people and animals you encounter. For example, if you greet a friend warmly, he will be happy to greet the person as well. If, however, you are hesitant or anxious about the approach of a stranger, he will respond accordingly.

Once the puppy begins to produce hormones, his natural curiosity emerges and he begins to investigate the world around him. It is at this time when you may notice that the untrained dog begins to wander away from you and even ignore your commands to stay close. When this behavior becomes a problem, the owner has two choices: get rid of the dog or train him. It is strongly urged that you choose the latter option.

There are usually training classes within a reasonable distance from your home, but you also do a lot to train your dog yourself. Sometimes there are classes available but the tuition is too costly. Whatever the circumstances, the solution to training your Great Dane without formal lessons lies within the pages of this book.

This chapter is devoted to helping you train your Great Dane at home. If the recommended procedures are followed faithfully, you may expect positive results that will prove rewarding to both you and your dog.

Whether your new charge is a puppy or a mature adult, the methods of teaching and the techniques we use in training basic behaviors are the same. After all, no dog, whether puppy or adult, likes harsh or inhumane methods. All creatures, however, respond favorably to gentle motivational methods and sincere praise and encouragement. Now let us get started.

HOUSEBREAKING

You can train a puppy to relieve himself wherever you choose, but this must be somewhere suitable. You should bear in mind from the outset that when your puppy is old enough to go out in public places, any canine deposits must be removed at once. You will always have to carry with you a plastic bag or "poop-scoop."

Outdoor training includes such surfaces as grass, dirt or

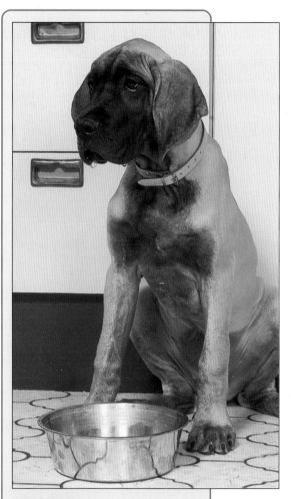

MEALTIME
Mealtime should be a peaceful time for your puppy. Do not put his food and water bowls in a high-traffic area in the house. For example, give him his own little corner of the kitchen where he can eat undisturbed and where he will not be underfoot. Do not allow small children or other family members to disturb the pup when he is eating.

You can purchase a tool from your local pet shop to assist you in cleaning up after your dog relieves himself.

PUPPY'S NEEDS

The puppy needs to relieve himself after play periods, after each meal, after he has been sleeping and any time he indicates that he is looking for a place to urinate or defecate. The urinary and intestinal tract muscles of very young puppies are not fully developed. Therefore, like human babies, puppies need to relieve themselves frequently.

Take your puppy out often—every hour for an eight-week-old, for example, and always

cement. Indoor training usually means training your dog to newspaper, *not* a viable option with a giant breed!

When deciding on the surface and location that you will want your Great Dane to use, be sure it is going to be permanent. Training your dog to grass and then changing your mind two months later is extremely difficult for both dog and owner.

Next, choose the command you will use each and every time you want your puppy to void. "Let's go" and "Hurry up" are examples of commands commonly used by dog owners.

Get in the habit of giving the puppy your chosen relief command before you take him out. That way, when he becomes an adult, you will be able to determine if he wants to go out when you ask him. A confirmation will be signs of interest such as wagging his tail, watching you intently, going to the door, etc.

HONOR AND OBEY

Dogs are the most honorable animals in existence. They consider another species (humans) as their own. They interface with you. You are their leader. Puppies perceive children to be on their level; their actions around small children are different from their behavior around their adult masters.

CANINE DEVELOPMENT SCHEDULE

It is important to understand how and at what age a puppy develops into adulthood. If you are a puppy owner, consult the following Canine Development Schedule to determine the stage of development your puppy is currently experiencing. This knowledge will help you as you work with the puppy in the weeks and months ahead.

Period	Age	Characteristics
FIRST TO THIRD	**BIRTH TO SEVEN WEEKS**	Puppy needs food, sleep and warmth, and responds to simple and gentle touching. Needs mother for security and disciplining. Needs littermates for learning and interacting with other dogs. Pup learns to function within a pack and learns pack order of dominance. Begin socializing pup with adults and children for short periods. Pup begins to become aware of his environment.
FOURTH	**EIGHT TO TWELVE WEEKS**	Brain is fully developed. Needs socializing with outside world. Remove from mother and littermates. Needs to change from canine pack to human pack. Human dominance necessary. Fear period occurs between 8 and 16 weeks. Avoid fright and pain.
FIFTH	**THIRTEEN TO SIXTEEN WEEKS**	Training and formal obedience should begin. Less association with other dogs, more with people, places, situations. Period will pass easily if you remember this is pup's change-to-adolescence time. Be firm and fair. Flight instinct prominent. Permissiveness and over-disciplining can do permanent damage. Praise for good behavior.
JUVENILE	**FOUR TO EIGHT MONTHS**	Another fear period about 7 to 8 months of age. It passes quickly, but be cautious of fright and pain. Sexual maturity reached. Dominant traits established. Dog should understand sit, down, come and stay by now.

NOTE: THESE ARE APPROXIMATE TIME FRAMES. ALLOW FOR INDIVIDUAL DIFFERENCES IN PUPPIES.

TAKE THE LEAD

Do not carry your dog to his relief area. Lead him there on a leash or, better yet, encourage him to follow you to the spot. If you start carrying him to his spot, you might end up doing this routine forever and your dog will have the satisfaction of having trained *you*.

immediately after sleeping and eating. The older the puppy, the less often he will need to relieve himself. Finally, as a mature healthy adult, he will require only three to five relief trips per day.

HOUSING

Since the types of housing and control you provide for your puppy have a direct relationship on the success of housebreaking, we consider the various aspects of both before we begin training.

Bringing a new puppy home and turning him loose in your house can be compared to turning a child loose in a sports arena and telling the child that the place is all his! The sheer enormity of the place would be too much for him to handle.

Instead, offer the puppy clearly defined areas where he can

Your house-trained Great Dane will know the routine and reliably use his chosen relief site.

play, sleep, eat and live. A room of the house where the family gathers is the most obvious choice. Puppies are social animals and need to feel a part of the pack right from the start. Hearing your voice, watching you while you are doing things and smelling you nearby are all positive reinforcers that he is now a member of your pack. Usually a family room, the kitchen or a nearby adjoining breakfast area is ideal for providing safety and security for both puppy and owner.

Within that room, there should be a smaller area that the puppy can call his own. An alcove, a wire or fiberglass dog crate or a fenced (not boarded!) corner from which he can view the activities of his new family

The best way to develop well-behaved adult dogs is to reward pups for polite behavior starting at a young age.

OPEN MINDS

Dogs are as different from each other as people are. What works for one dog may not work for another. Have an open mind. If one method of training is unsuccessful, try another.

PAPER CAPER

Never line your pup's sleeping area with newspaper. Puppy litters are usually raised on newspaper and, once in your home, the puppy will immediately associate newspaper with voiding. Never put newspaper on any floor while housebreaking, as this will only confuse the puppy. Finally, restrict water intake after evening meals. Offer a few licks at a time—never let a young puppy gulp water after meals; gulping water is not good for adult dogs, either.

will be fine. The size of the area or crate is the key factor here. The area must be large enough for the puppy to lie down and stretch out as well as stand up without rubbing his head on the top, yet divided into a small enough section that he cannot relieve himself at one end and sleep at the other without coming into contact with his droppings during the housebreaking process.

The designated area should be lined with clean bedding and contain a toy. Do not put food or

THE SUCCESS METHOD

1 Tell the puppy "Crate time!" and place him in the crate with a small treat (a piece of cheese or half of a biscuit). Let him stay in the crate for five minutes while you are in the same room. Then release him and praise lavishly. Never release him when he is fussing. Wait until he is quiet before you let him out.

2 Repeat Step 1 several times a day.

3 The next day, place the puppy in the crate as before. Let him stay there for ten minutes. Do this several times.

4 Continue building time in five-minute increments until the puppy

stays in his crate for 30 minutes with you in the room. Always take him to his relief area after prolonged periods in his crate.

5 Now go back to Step 1 and let the puppy stay in his crate for five minutes, this time while you are out of the room.

6 Once again, build crate time in five-minute increments with you out of the room. When the puppy will stay willingly in his crate (he may even fall asleep!) for 30 minutes with you out of the room, he will be ready to stay in it for several hours at a time.

water in the dog's crate during housebreaking, as eating and drinking will activate his digestive processes and ultimately defeat your purpose if the pup always has "to go."

Dogs are, by nature, clean animals and will not remain close to their relief areas unless forced to do so. In those cases, they then become dirty dogs and usually remain that way for life.

CONTROL

By *control*, we mean helping the puppy to create a lifestyle pattern that will be compatible to that of his human pack (you!). Just as we guide little children to learn our way of life, we must show the puppy when it is time to play, eat, sleep, exercise and even entertain himself.

Your puppy should always sleep in his crate. He should also learn that, during times of household confusion and excessive human activity such as at breakfast when family members are preparing for the day, he can play by himself in relative safety and comfort in his designated area. Each time you leave the puppy alone, he should understand exactly where he is to stay.

Puppies are chewers. They cannot tell the difference between lamp cords, television wires, shoes, table legs, etc. Chewing into a television wire, for example, can be fatal to the puppy,

HOW MANY TIMES A DAY?

AGE	RELIEF TRIPS
To 14 weeks	10
14–22 weeks	8
22–32 weeks	6
Adulthood	4
(dog stops growing)	

These are estimates, of course, but they are a guide to the *minimum* number of opportunities a dog should have each day to relieve himself.

while a shorted wire can start a fire in the house.

If the puppy chews on the arm of the chair when he is alone, you will probably discipline him angrily when you get home. Thus, he makes the association that your coming home means he is going to be punished. (He will not remember chewing the chair and is inca-

TRAINING RULES

If you want to be successful in training your dog, you have four rules to obey yourself:

1. Develop an understanding of how a dog thinks.
2. Do not blame the dog for lack of communication.
3. Define your dog's personality and act accordingly.
4. Have patience and be consistent.

pable of making the association of the discipline with his naughty deed.)

Times of excitement, such as visits from friends, family parties, etc., can be fun for the puppy, providing he can view the activities from the security of his designated area. He is not underfoot and he is not being fed all sorts of tidbits that will probably cause him stomach distress, yet he still feels a part of the fun. The foregoing are just a few examples of situations in which crating the pup will keep him safe and will encourage proper behavior by keeping him out of trouble.

SCHEDULE

A puppy should be taken to his relief area each time he is released from his designated area, after meals, after play sessions, when he first awakens in the morning (at age eight weeks, this can mean 5 a.m.!). The puppy will indicate that he's ready "to go" by circling or sniffing busily—do not ignore or misinterpret these signs. For a puppy less than ten weeks of age, a routine of taking him out every hour is necessary. As the puppy grows, he will be able to wait for longer periods of time.

Keep trips to his relief area short. Stay no more than five or six minutes and then return to the house. If he goes during that time, praise him lavishly and take him indoors immediately. If he does

Most litters are raised on newspapers, and this is the surface on which they relieve themselves when very young. Some breeders will start training the pups to go outdoors before they go to new owners, which is obviously to the new owners' advantage.

not, but he has an accident when you go back indoors, pick him up immediately, say "No! No!" and return to his relief area. Wait a few minutes, then return to the house again. Never hit a puppy or put his face in urine or excrement when he has an accident!

Once indoors, put the puppy in his crate until you have had time to clean up his accident. Then release him to the family area and watch him more closely than before. Chances are, his accident was a result of your not picking up his signal or waiting too

long before offering him the opportunity to relieve himself. Never hold a grudge against the puppy for accidents.

Let the puppy learn that going outdoors means it is time to relieve himself, not to play. Once trained, he will be able to play indoors and out and still differentiate between the times for play versus the times for relief.

Help him develop regular hours for naps, being alone, playing by himself and just resting, all in his crate. Encourage him to entertain himself while you are

KEEP SMILING
Never train your dog, puppy or adult, when you are angry or in a sour mood. Dogs are very sensitive to human feelings, especially anger, and if your dog senses that you are angry or upset, he will connect your anger with his training and learn to resent or fear his training sessions.

busy with your activities. Let him learn that having you near is comforting, but it is not your main purpose in life to provide him with undivided attention.

Each time you put your puppy in his own area, use the same command, whatever suits best. Soon, he will run to his crate or special area when he hears you say those words.

Crate training provides safety for you, the puppy and the home. It also provides the puppy with a feeling of security, and that helps the puppy achieve self-confidence and clean habits.

Remember that one of the primary ingredients in housebreaking your puppy is control. Regardless of your lifestyle, there will always be occasions when you will need to have a place where your dog can stay and be happy and safe. Crate training is the answer for now and in the future.

In conclusion, a few key elements are really all you need for a successful housebreaking method—consistency, frequency, praise, control and supervision. By following these procedures with a normal healthy puppy, you and the puppy will soon be past the stage of "accidents" and ready to move on to a full and rewarding life together.

ROLES OF DISCIPLINE, REWARD AND PUNISHMENT
Discipline, training one to act in accordance with rules, brings order to life. It is as simple as that. Without discipline, particularly in a group society, chaos reigns supreme and the group will eventually perish. Humans and canines are social animals and need some form of discipline in order to function effectively. They must procure food, reproduce to keep the species going and protect their home base and their young.

If there were no discipline in the lives of social animals, they would eventually die from starvation and/or predation by other stronger animals. In the case of domestic canines, dogs need discipline in their lives in order to understand how their pack (you and other family members) functions and how they must act in order to survive.

A large humane society in a highly populated area recently surveyed dog owners regarding their satisfaction with their relationships with their dogs. People who had trained their dogs were 75% more satisfied with their pets than those who had never trained their dogs.

Dr. Edward Thorndike, a psychologist, established *Thorndike's Theory of Learning*, which states that a behavior that results in a pleasant event tends to be repeated. A behavior that results in an unpleasant event tends not to be repeated. It is this theory on which training methods are based today. For example, if you manipulate a dog to perform a specific behavior and reward him for doing it, he is likely to do it again because he enjoyed the end result.

Occasionally, punishment, a penalty inflicted for an offense, is necessary. The best type of punishment often comes from an outside source. For example, a child is told not to touch the stove because he may get burned. He disobeys and touches the stove. In doing so, he receives a burn. From that time on, he respects the heat of the stove and avoids contact with it. Therefore, a behavior that results in an unpleasant event tends not to be repeated.

A good example of a dog learning the hard way is the dog who chases the house cat. He is told many times to leave the cat alone, yet he persists in teasing the cat. Then, one day he begins chasing the cat but the cat turns

PRACTICE MAKES PERFECT!
- Have training lessons with your dog every day in several short segments—three to five times a day for a few minutes at a time is ideal.
- Do not have long practice sessions. The dog will become easily bored.
- Never practice when you are tired, ill, worried or in an otherwise negative mood. This will transmit to the dog and may have an adverse effect on his performance.

Think fun, short and above all *positive!* End each session on a high note, rather than a failed exercise, and make sure to give a lot of praise. Enjoy the training and help your dog enjoy it, too.

LANGUAGE BARRIER

Dogs do not understand our language and have to rely on tone of voice more than just words or sound. They can be trained to react to a certain sound, at a certain volume. If you say "No, Oliver" in a very soft, pleasant voice, it will not have the same meaning as "No, Oliver!!" when you raise your voice.

You should never use the dog's name during a reprimand, just the command "No!" You never want the dog to associate his name with a negative experience or reprimand.

and swipes a claw across the dog's face, leaving him with a painful gash on his nose. The final result is that the dog stops chasing the cat.

TRAINING EQUIPMENT

COLLAR AND LEASH

For a Great Dane, the collar and leash that you use for training must be one with which you are easily able to work, comfortable for the dog and perfectly safe.

TREATS

Have a bag of treats on hand. Something nutritious and easy to swallow works best. Use a soft treat, a chunk of cheese or a piece of cooked chicken rather than a dry biscuit. By the time the dog has finished chewing a dry treat,

he will forget why he is being rewarded in the first place! Using food rewards will not teach a dog to beg at the table—the only way to teach a dog to beg at the table is to give him food from the table. In training, rewarding the dog with a food treat will help him associate praise and the treats with learning new behaviors that obviously please his owner.

TRAINING BEGINS: ASK THE DOG A QUESTION

In order to teach your dog anything, you must first get his attention. After all, he cannot learn anything if he is looking away from you with his mind on something else.

To get his attention, ask him "School?" and immediately walk over to him and give him a treat as you tell him "Good dog." Wait a minute or two and repeat the routine, this time with a treat in your hand as you approach within a foot of the dog. Do not go directly to him, but stop about a foot short of him and hold out the treat as you ask "School?" He will see you approaching with a treat in your hand and most likely begin walking toward you. As you meet, give him the treat and praise again.

The third time, ask the question, have a treat in your hand and walk only a short distance toward the dog so that he must walk almost all the way to you.

As he reaches you, give him the treat and praise again.

By this time, the dog will probably be getting the idea that if he pays attention to you, especially when you ask that question, it will pay off in treats and enjoyable activities for him. In other words, he learns that "school" means doing activities with you that result in treats and positive attention for him.

Remember that the dog does not understand your verbal language, he only recognizes sounds. Your question translates to a series of sounds for him, and those sounds become the signal to go to you and pay attention; if he does, he will get to interact with you plus receive treats and praise.

THE BASIC COMMANDS

TEACHING SIT

Now that you have the dog's attention, attach his leash and hold it in your left hand and a food treat in your right. Place your food hand at the dog's nose and let him lick the treat but not take it from you. Say "Sit" and slowly raise your food hand from in front of the pup's nose up over his head so that he is looking at the ceiling. As he bends his head upward, he should have to bend his knees to maintain his balance. As he bends his knees, he will assume a sit position. At that point, release the food treat and

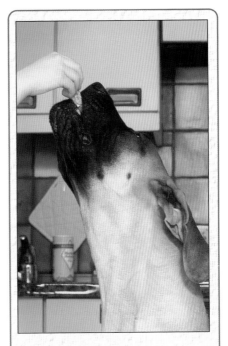

HOW TO WEAN THE "TREAT HOG"

If you have trained your dog by rewarding him with a treat each time he performs a command, he may soon decide that without the treat, he won't sit, stay or come. The best way to fix this problem is to start asking your dog to do certain commands twice before being rewarded. Slowly increase the number of commands given and then vary the number: three sits and a treat one day, five sits for a biscuit the next day, etc. Your dog will soon realize that there is no set number of sits before he gets his reward and he'll likely do it the first time you ask in the hope of being rewarded sooner rather than later.

will wean him off the food treats but still maintain the verbal praise. After all, you will always have your voice with you, and there will be many times when you have no food rewards but expect the dog to obey.

TEACHING DOWN

Teaching the down exercise is easy when you understand how the dog perceives the down position, and it is very difficult when you do not. Dogs perceive the down position as a submissive one. Teaching the down exercise using a forceful method can sometimes make the dog develop such a fear of the down that he either runs away when you say "Down" or he attempts to snap at the person who tries to force him down.

Have the dog sit close alongside your left leg, facing in the same direction as you are. Hold the leash in your left hand and a food treat in your right. Now place your left hand lightly on

A polite pair sitting pretty—blue adult and harlequin puppy.

praise lavishly with comments such as "Good dog! Good sit!" etc. Remember to always praise enthusiastically, because dogs relish verbal praise from their owners and feel so proud of themselves whenever they accomplish a behavior.

You will not use food forever in getting the dog to obey your commands. Food is only used to teach new behaviors, and once the dog knows what you want when you give a specific command, you

DOUBLE JEOPARDY

A dog in jeopardy never lies down. He stays alert on his feet because instinct tells him that he may have to run away or fight for his survival. Therefore, if a dog feels threatened or anxious, he will not lie down. Consequently, it is important to keep the dog calm and relaxed as he learns the down exercise.

the top of the dog's shoulders where they meet above the spinal cord. Do not push down on the dog's shoulders; simply rest your left hand there so you can guide the dog to lie down close to your left leg rather than to swing away from your side when he drops.

Now place the food hand at the dog's nose, say "Down" very softly (almost a whisper) and slowly lower the food hand to the dog's front feet. When the food hand reaches the floor, begin moving it forward along the floor in front of the dog. Keep talking softly to the dog, saying things like, "Do you want this treat? You can do this, good dog." Your reassuring tone of voice will help calm the dog as he tries to follow the food hand in order to get the treat.

When the dog's elbows touch the floor, release the food and praise softly. Try to get the dog to maintain that down position for several seconds before you let him sit up again. The goal here is to get the dog to settle down and not feel threatened in the down position.

TEACHING STAY

It is easy to teach the dog to stay in either a sit or a down position. Again, we use food and praise during the teaching process as we help the dog to understand exactly what it is that we are expecting him to do.

To teach the sit/stay, start with the dog sitting on your left side as before and hold the leash in your left hand. Have a food treat in your right hand and place your food hand at the dog's nose. Say "Stay" and step out on your right foot to stand directly in front of the dog, toe to toe, as he licks and nibbles the treat. Be sure to keep his head facing upward to maintain the sit position. Count to five and then swing around to stand next to the dog again with him on your left. As soon as you get back to the original position, release the food and praise lavishly.

To teach the down/stay, do the down as previously described. As soon as the dog lies down, say "Stay" and step out on your right foot just as you did in the sit/stay.

CONSISTENCY PAYS OFF

Dogs need consistency in their feeding schedule, exercise and relief visits, and in the verbal commands you use. If you use "Stay" on Monday and "Stay here, please" on Tuesday, you will confuse your dog. Don't demand perfect behavior during training sessions and then let him have the run of the house the rest of the day. Above all, lavish praise on your pet consistently every time he does something right. The more he feels he is pleasing you, the more willing he will be to learn.

The down position is not as simple to teach as the sit position. The down is a submissive posture for dogs, and one that they may not be too eager to assume unless they are at ease.

Count to five and then return to stand beside the dog with him on your left side. Release the treat and praise as always.

Within a week or ten days, you can begin to add a bit of

COMMAND STANCE
Stand up straight and authoritatively when giving your dog commands. Do not issue commands when lying on the floor or lying on your back on the sofa. If you are on your hands and knees when you give a command, your dog will think you are positioning yourself to play.

distance between you and your dog when you leave him. When you do, use your left hand open with the palm facing the dog as a stay signal, much the same as the hand signal a police officer uses to stop traffic at an intersection. Hold the food treat in your right hand as before, but this time the food is not touching the dog's nose. He will watch the food hand and quickly learn that he is going to get that treat as soon as you return to his side.

When you can stand 3 feet away from your dog for 30 seconds, you can then begin

"COME" . . . BACK

Never call your dog to come to you for a correction or scold him when he reaches you. That is the quickest way to turn a "Come" into "Go away fast!" Dogs think only in the present tense, and your dog will connect the scolding with coming to you, not with the misbehavior of a few moments earlier.

building time and distance in both stays. Eventually, the dog can be expected to remain in the stay position for prolonged periods of time until you return to him or call him to you. Always praise lavishly when he stays.

TEACHING COME

If you make teaching "come" a fun experience, you should never have a student that does not love the game or that fails to come when called. The secret, it seems, is never to teach the word "come."

At times when an owner most wants his dog to come when called, the owner is likely upset or anxious and he allows these feelings to come through in the tone of his voice when he calls his dog. Hearing that desperation in his owner's voice, the dog fears the results of going to him and therefore either disobeys outright or runs in the opposite direction. The secret, therefore, is to teach the dog a game and, when you

want him to come to you, simply play the game. It is practically a no-fail solution!

To begin, have several members of your family take a few food treats and each go into a different room in the house. Take turns calling the dog, and each person should celebrate the dog's finding him with a treat and lots of happy praise. When a person calls the dog, he is actually inviting the dog to find him and get a treat as a reward for "winning."

A few turns of the "Where are you?" game and the dog will understand that everyone is playing the game and that each person has a big celebration awaiting the dog's success at locating him. Once the dog learns to love the game, simply calling out "Where are you?" will bring him running from wherever he is when he hears that all-important question.

The come command is recognized as one of the most impor-

"I'm right here!" Your dog should always answer your "Where are you?" question by coming to you.

tant things to teach a dog, but there are trainers who work with thousands of dogs and never teach the actual word "come." Yet these dogs will race to respond to a person who uses the dog's name followed by "Where are you?" For example, a woman has a 12-year-old companion dog who went blind, but who never fails to locate her owner when asked, "Where are you?"

Children particularly love to play this game with their dogs. Children can hide in smaller places like a shower stall or bathtub, behind a bed or under a table. The dog needs to work a little bit harder to find these

hiding places but, when he does, he loves to celebrate with a treat and a tussle with a favorite youngster.

TEACHING HEEL

Heeling means that the dog walks beside the owner without pulling. It takes time and patience on the owner's part to succeed at teaching the dog that he (the owner) will not proceed unless the dog is walking calmly beside him. Pulling out ahead on the leash is definitely not acceptable.

Begin with holding the leash in your left hand as the dog sits beside your left leg. Move the loop end of the leash to your right hand but keep your left hand short on the leash so it keeps the dog in close next to you.

Say "Heel" and step forward on your left foot. Keep the dog close to you and take three steps. Stop and have the dog sit next to you in what we now call the heel position. Praise verbally, but do not touch the dog. Hesitate a moment and begin again with

HEELING WELL
Teach your dog to heel in an enclosed area. Once you think the dog will obey reliably and you want to attempt advanced obedience exercises such as off-lead heeling, test him in a fenced-in area so he cannot run away.

Once a dog is reliably obedience trained, you can move on to more advanced activities. Find what your Great Dane enjoys and have some fun!

"Heel," taking three steps and stopping, at which point the dog is told to sit again.

Your goal here is to have the dog walk those three steps without pulling on the leash. When he will walk calmly beside you for three steps without pulling, increase the number of steps you take to five. When he will walk politely beside you while you take five steps, you can increase the length of your walk to ten steps. Keep increasing the length of your stroll until the dog will walk quietly beside you without pulling as long as you want him to heel. When you stop heeling, indicate to the dog that the exercise is over by verbally praising as you pet him and say "OK, good dog." The "OK" is used as a release word, meaning that the exercise is finished and the dog is free to relax.

If you are dealing with a dog who insists on pulling you around, simply "put on your brakes" and stand your ground until the dog realizes that the two of you are not going anywhere until he is beside you and moving at your pace, not his. It may take some time just standing there to convince the dog that you are the leader and you will be the one to

TRAINING TIP

If you are walking your dog and he suddenly stops and looks straight into your eyes, ignore him. Pull the leash and lead him into the direction you want to walk.

A dog as large as the Great Dane must be trained to heel at his owner's side. It is simply not possible to walk an untrained Dane.

decide on the direction and speed of your travel.

Each time the dog looks up at you or slows down to give a slack leash between the two of you, quietly praise him and say, "Good heel. Good dog." Eventually, the dog will begin to respond and within a few days he will be walking politely beside you without pulling on the leash. At first, the training sessions should be kept short and very positive; soon the dog will

be able to walk nicely with you for increasingly longer distances. Remember also to give the dog free time and the opportunity to run and play when you have finished heel practice.

WEANING OFF FOOD IN TRAINING

Food is used in training new behaviors. Once the dog understands what behavior goes with a specific command, it is time to start weaning him off the food treats. At first, give a treat after each exercise. Then, start to give a treat only after every other exercise. Vary the times when you offer a food reward and the times when you only offer praise so that the dog will never know when he is going to receive both food and praise and when he is going to receive only praise. This is called a variable ratio reward system and it proves successful because there is always the chance that the owner will produce a treat, so the dog never stops trying for that reward. No matter what, *always* give verbal praise.

OBEDIENCE CLASSES

It is a good idea to enroll in an obedience class if one is available in your area. If yours is a show dog, handling classes to prepare for the show ring would be more appropriate. Many areas have dog clubs that offer basic

Consider classes to learn the etiquette of the show ring if your Great Dane is show-quality and you'd like to try your hand at showing.

obedience training as well as preparatory classes for competition. There are also local dog trainers who offer similar classes.

> **ATTENTION!**
> Your dog is actually training you at the same time you are training him. Dogs do things to get attention. They usually repeat whatever succeeds in getting your attention.

At obedience trials, dogs can earn titles at various levels of competition. The beginning levels of competition include basic behaviors such as sit, down, heel, etc. The more advanced levels of competition include jumping, retrieving, scent discrimination and signal work. The advanced levels require a dog and owner to put a lot of time and effort into their training and the titles that can be earned at these levels of competition are very prestigious.

OTHER ACTIVITIES FOR LIFE

Whether a dog is trained in the structured environment of a class or alone with his owner at home, there are many activities that can bring fun and rewards to both owner and dog once they have mastered basic control.

Teaching the dog to help out around the home, in the garden or on the farm provides great satis-faction to both dog and owner. In addition, the dog's help makes life a little easier for his owner and raises his stature as a valued companion to his family. It helps give the dog a purpose by occupy-ing his mind and providing an outlet for his energy.

Backpacking is an exciting and healthy activity that the dog can be taught without assistance from more than his owner. The exercise of walking and climbing is good for man and dog alike, and the bond that they develop together is priceless. The rule of thumb for backpacking is never to allow the dog to carry more than one-sixth of his body weight.

If you are interested in partici-pating in organized competition with your Great Dane, there are activities other than obedience in which you and your dog can become involved. Agility is a popular sport in which dogs run through an obstacle course that includes various jumps, tunnels and other exercises to test the dog's speed and coordination. The owners run through the course beside their dogs to give commands and to guide them through the course. Although competitive, the focus is on fun—it's fun to do, fun to watch and great exercise.

THE STUDENT'S STRESS TEST

During training sessions, you must be able to recognize signs of stress in your dog such as:
- tucking his tail between his legs
- lowering his head
- shivering or trembling
- standing completely still or running away
- panting and/or salivating
- avoiding eye contact
- flattening his ears back
- urinating submissively
- rolling over and lifting a leg
- grinning or baring teeth
- aggression when restrained

If your four-legged student displays these signs, he may just be nervous or intimidated. The training session may have been too lengthy, with not enough praise and affirmation. Stop for the day and try again tomorrow.

Many Great Danes have a passion for swimming. If your Great Dane is going to "test the waters," make sure the swimming area is safe and that he is always supervised.

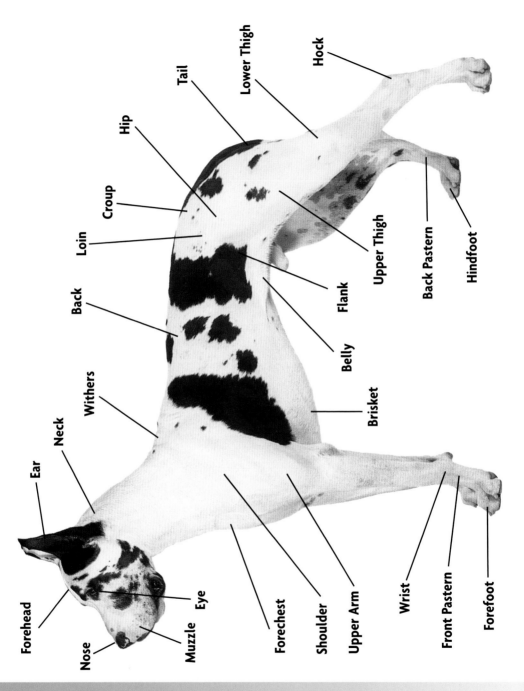

Physical Structure of the Great Dane

Tail

Lower Thigh

Hock

Hip

Croup

Upper Thigh

Loin

Back Pastern

Hindfoot

Back

Flank

Withers

Belly

Neck

Brisket

Ear

Forehead

Nose

Eye

Muzzle

Forechest

Shoulder

Upper Arm

Wrist

Front Pastern

Forefoot

Dogs suffer from many of the same physical illnesses as people. They might even share many of the same psychological problems. Since people usually know more about human diseases than canine maladies, many of the terms used in this chapter will be familiar but not necessarily those used by vets. We will use the term *x-ray*, instead of the more acceptable term *radiograph*. We will also use the familiar term *symptoms* even though dogs don't have symptoms, which are verbal descriptions of the patient's feelings; dogs have *clinical signs*. Since dogs can't speak, we have to look for clinical signs... but we still use the term *symptoms* in this book.

As a general rule, medicine is *practiced*. That term is not arbitrary. Medicine is a constantly changing art as we learn more and more about genetics, electronic aids (like CAT scans and MRIs) and daily laboratory advances. There are many dog maladies, like canine hip dysplasia, which are not universally treated in the same manner. Some vets opt for surgery more often than others do.

Before you buy your Great Dane puppy, meet and interview the vets in your area. Take everything into consideration; discuss his background, specialties, fees, office hours, emergency policy, etc.

SELECTING A QUALIFIED VET

Your selection of a veterinarian should be based not only upon his personality but also upon his skills and experience with giant-breed dogs and his convenience to your home. You want a vet who is close by because you might have emergencies or need to make multiple visits for treatments. You want a vet who has services that you might require such as tattooing and possibly boarding facilities, as well as pet supplies and a good reputation for ability and responsiveness. There is nothing more frustrating than having to wait a day or more to get a response from your vet.

A typical vet's income, categorized according to services performed. This survey dealt with small-animal (pets) practices.

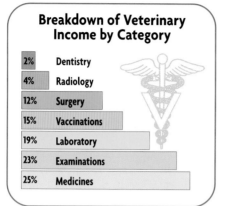

Breakdown of Veterinary Income by Category

%	Category
2%	Dentistry
4%	Radiology
12%	Surgery
15%	Vaccinations
19%	Laboratory
23%	Examinations
25%	Medicines

All vets are licensed and their diplomas and/or certificates should be displayed in their waiting rooms. Most vets do routine surgery such as neutering, stitching up wounds and docking tails for those breeds in which such is required for show purposes. There are, however, many veterinary specialties that require further studies and internships. There are specialists in heart problems (veterinary cardiologists), skin problems (veterinary dermatologists), teeth and gum problems (veterinary dentists), eye problems (veterinary ophthalmologists) and x-rays (veterinary radiologists), as well as vets who have specialties in bones, muscles or certain organs.

When the problem affecting your dog is serious, it is not unusual or impudent to get another medical opinion, although it is courteous to advise the vets concerned about this. You might also want to compare costs among several vets. Sophisticated health care and veterinary services can be very costly. If various treatments are available, cost can be an important factor in deciding upon the course of treatment to take.

PREVENTATIVE MEDICINE
It is much easier, less costly and more effective to practice preventative medicine than to fight bouts of illness and disease. Properly bred puppies come from parents who were selected based upon their genetic-disease profiles. Their mother should have been vaccinated, free of all internal and external parasites and properly nourished. For these reasons, a visit to the vet who cared for the dam is recommended. The dam can pass on disease resistance to her puppies, which can last for eight to ten weeks. She can also pass on parasites and many infections. That's why it's helpful to know as much as possible about the dam's health.

VACCINATION SCHEDULING
Most vaccinations are given by injection and should only be done by a vet. Both he and you should keep a record of the date of the injection, the identification of the vaccine and the amount given. Some vets give a first vaccination at eight weeks, but most dog breeders prefer the course not to commence until about ten weeks

because of the risk of negating any antibodies passed on by the dam. The vaccination scheduling is usually based on a 15-day cycle. You must take your vet's advice regarding when to vaccinate, as this may differ according to the vaccine used.

Most vaccinations immunize your puppy against viruses. The usual vaccines contain immunizing doses of several different viruses such as distemper, parvovirus, parainfluenza and hepatitis, although some vets recommend separate vaccines for each disease. There are other vaccines available when the puppy is at risk. You should rely upon professional advice. This is especially true for the booster-shot program. Most vaccination programs require a booster when the puppy is a year old and once a year thereafter. In some cases, circumstances may require more or less frequent immunizations. Kennel cough, more formally known as tracheobronchitis, is treated with a vaccine that is sprayed into the dog's nostrils. Kennel cough is usually included in routine vaccination, but this is often not as effective as for other major diseases.

WEANING TO FIVE MONTHS OLD

Puppies should be weaned by the time they are about two months old. A puppy that remains for at least eight weeks with his mother and littermates usually adapts better to other dogs and people later in life.

New owners should have their puppy examined by a vet immediately, either before bringing the pup home or within a day or two after. The puppy will have his teeth examined and have his skeletal conformation and general health checked prior to certification by the vet. Puppies in certain breeds may have problems with their kneecaps, cataracts and other eye problems, heart murmurs and undescended testicles. They may also have personality problems and your vet might have training in temperament evaluation. During the first visit, your vet will also set up a schedule for your pup's vaccinations.

FIVE TO TWELVE MONTHS OF AGE

Unless you intend to breed or show your dog, neutering the puppy around six months of age is recommended and likely required in the breeder's sales contract. Discuss this with your vet. Neutering and spaying have proven to be extremely beneficial

> **AVOID SUPPLEMENTATION**
> Discuss the dangers of vitamin and mineral supplementation with your veterinarian. Calcium supplements, for example, can lead to bone deformities that can cripple Great Danes. Never initiate any supplementation without first consulting your vet.

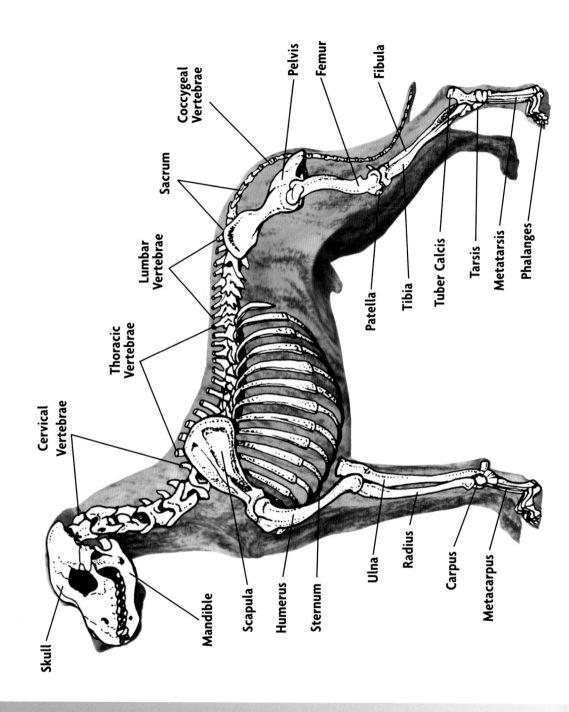

Skeletal Structure of the Great Dane

Coccygeal Vertebrae

Pelvis

Femur

Fibula

Sacrum

Lumbar Vertebrae

Thoracic Vertebrae

Patella

Tibia

Tuber Calcis

Tarsis

Metatarsis

Phalanges

Cervical Vertebrae

Skull

Mandible

Scapula

Humerus

Sternum

Ulna

Radius

Carpus

Metacarpus

to male and female dogs, respectively. Besides eliminating the possibility of pregnancy, it inhibits (but does not prevent) breast cancer in bitches and prostate cancer in male dogs.

Your vet should provide your puppy with a thorough dental evaluation at six months of age, ascertaining whether all of the permanent teeth have erupted properly. A home dental-care regimen should be initiated at six months, including brushing weekly and providing good dental devices (such as nylon bones). Regular dental care promotes healthy teeth, fresh breath and a longer life.

OLDER THAN ONE YEAR
Once a year, your grown dog should visit the vet for an examination and vaccination boosters, if needed. Some vets recommend blood tests, thyroid level check and dental evaluation to accompany these annual visits. A thorough clinical evaluation by the vet can provide critical background information for your dog. Blood tests are often performed at one year of age, and dental examinations around the third or fourth

HEALTH AND VACCINATION SCHEDULE

AGE IN WEEKS:	6TH	8TH	10TH	12TH	14TH	16TH	20-24TH	52ND
Worm Control	✔	✔	✔	✔	✔	✔	✔	
Neutering								✔
Heartworm		✔		✔		✔	✔	
Parvovirus	✔		✔		✔		✔	✔
Distemper		✔		✔		✔		✔
Hepatitis		✔		✔		✔		✔
Leptospirosis								✔
Parainfluenza	✔		✔		✔			✔
Dental Examination		✔					✔	✔
Complete Physical		✔					✔	✔
Coronavirus				✔			✔	✔
Kennel Cough	✔							
Hip Dysplasia								✔
Rabies							✔	

Vaccinations are not instantly effective. It takes about two weeks for the dog's immune system to develop antibodies. Most vaccinations require annual booster shots. Your vet should guide you in this regard.

First Aid at a Glance

Burns
Place the affected area under cool water; use ice if only a small area is burnt.

Bee stings/Insect bites
Apply ice to relieve swelling; antihistamine dosed properly.

Animal bites
Clean any bleeding area; apply pressure until bleeding subsides; go to the vet.

Spider bites
Use cold compress and a pressurized pack to inhibit venom's spreading.

Antifreeze poisoning
Induce vomiting with hydrogen peroxide. Seek *immediate* veterinary help!

Fish hooks
Removal best handled by vet; hook must be cut in order to remove.

Snake bites
Pack ice around bite; contact vet quickly; identify snake for proper antivenin.

Car accident
Move dog from roadway with blanket; seek veterinary aid.

Shock
Calm the dog; keep him warm; seek *immediate* veterinary help.

Nosebleed
Apply cold compress to the nose; apply pressure to any visible abrasion.

Bleeding
Apply pressure above the area; treat wound by applying a cotton pack.

Heat stroke
Submerge dog in cold bath; cool down with fresh air and water; go to the vet.

Frostbite/Hypothermia
Warm the dog with a warm bath, electric blankets or hot water bottles.

Abrasions
Clean the wound and wash out thoroughly with fresh water; apply antiseptic.

 Remember: an injured dog may attempt to bite a helping hand from fear and confusion. Always muzzle the dog before trying to offer assistance.

birthday. In the long run, quality preventative care for your pet can save money, teeth and lives.

SKIN PROBLEMS IN GREAT DANES

Vets are consulted by dog owners for skin problems more than for any other group of diseases or maladies. Dogs' skin is almost as sensitive as human skin and both suffer from almost the same ailments. For example, Great Danes often suffer from acne during puberty until about three years of age. For these reasons, veterinary dermatology has developed into a specialty practiced by many vets.

Since many skin problems have visual symptoms that are almost identical, it requires the skill of an experienced veterinary dermatologist to identify and cure many of the more severe skin disorders. Pet shops sell many treatments for skin problems, but most of the treatments are directed at symptoms and not the underlying problem(s). If your dog is suffering from a skin disorder,

DISEASE REFERENCE CHART

	What is it?	What causes it?	Symptoms
Leptospirosis	Severe disease that affects the internal organs; can be spread to people.	A bacterium, which is often carried by rodents, that enters through mucous membranes and spreads quickly throughout the body.	Range from fever, vomiting and loss of appetite in less severe cases to shock, irreversible kidney damage and possibly death in most severe cases.
Rabies	Potentially deadly virus that infects warm-blooded mammals.	Bite from a carrier of the virus, mainly wild animals.	1st stage: dog exhibits change in behavior, fear. 2nd stage: dog's behavior becomes more aggressive. 3rd stage: loss of coordination, trouble with bodily functions.
Parvovirus	Highly contagious virus, potentially deadly.	Ingestion of the virus, which is usually spread through the feces of infected dogs.	Most common: severe diarrhea. Also vomiting, fatigue, lack of appetite.
Kennel cough	Contagious respiratory infection.	Combination of types of bacteria and virus. Most common: *Bordetella bronchiseptica* bacteria and parainfluenza virus.	Chronic cough.
Distemper	Disease primarily affecting respiratory and nervous system.	Virus that is related to the human measles virus.	Mild symptoms such as fever, lack of appetite and mucus secretion progress to evidence of brain damage, "hard pad."
Hepatitis	Virus primarily affecting the liver.	Canine adenovirus type I (CAV-1). Enters system when dog breathes in particles.	Lesser symptoms include listlessness, diarrhea, vomiting. More severe symptoms include "blue-eye" (clumps of virus in eye).
Coronavirus	Virus resulting in digestive problems.	Virus is spread through infected dog's feces.	Stomach upset evidenced by lack of appetite, vomiting, diarrhea.

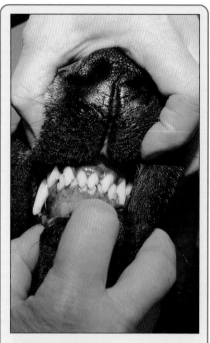

DENTAL HEALTH

A dental examination is in order when the dog is between six months and one year of age so that any permanent teeth that have erupted incorrectly can be corrected. It is important to begin a brushing routine at home, using either a toothbrush made for dogs or gauze wrapped around your finger, and canine toothpaste. Durable nylon and safe edible chews should be a part of your puppy's arsenal for good health, good teeth and pleasant breath. The vast majority of dogs three to four years old and older has diseases of the gums from lack of dental attention. Using the various types of dental chews can be very effective in controlling dental plaque.

you should seek professional assistance as quickly as possible. As with all diseases, the earlier a problem is identified and treated, the more likely it is that the cure will be successful.

HEREDITARY SKIN DISORDERS
Veterinary dermatologists are currently researching a number of skin disorders that are believed to have a hereditary basis. These inherited diseases are transmitted by both parents, who appear (phenotypically) normal but have a recessive gene for the disease, meaning that they carry, but are not affected by, the disease. These diseases pose serious problems to breeders because in some instances there are no methods of identifying carriers. Often the secondary diseases associated with these skin conditions are even more debilitating than the disorder itself, including cancers and respiratory problems.

Among the hereditary skin disorders, for which the mode of inheritance is known, are acrodermatitis, cutaneous asthenia (Ehlers-Danlos syndrome), sebaceous adenitis, cyclic hematopoiesis, dermatomyositis, IgA deficiency, color dilution alopecia and nodular dermatofibrosis. Some of these disorders are limited to one or two breeds and others affect a large number of breeds. Color dilution alopecia, for example, has been frequently seen in blue Great Danes. All inherited diseases must be diagnosed and treated by a veterinary specialist.

PARASITE BITES
Many of us are allergic to insect bites. The bites itch, erupt and may even become infected. Dogs have the same reaction to fleas, ticks and/or mites. When an insect lands on you, you have the chance to whisk it away with your hand. Unfortunately, when your dog is bitten by a flea, tick or mite, he can only scratch it away or bite it. By the time the dog has been bitten, the parasite has done some of its damage. It may also have laid eggs, which will cause further problems in the near future. The itching from parasite bites is probably due to the saliva injected into the site when the parasite sucks the dog's blood.

ACRAL LICK GRANULOMA
Many large dogs have a very poorly understood syndrome called acral lick granuloma, and the Great Dane is particularly prone. The manifestation of the problem is the dog's tireless attack at a specific area of the body, almost always the legs or paws. The dog licks so intensively that he removes the hair and skin, leaving an ugly, large wound. Tiny protuberances, which are outgrowths of new capillaries, bead on the surface of the wound. Owners who notice their dogs'

biting and chewing at their extremities should have the vet determine the cause. If lick granuloma is identified, although there is no absolute cure, corticosteroids are the most common treatment.

AIRBORNE ALLERGIES
Just as humans have hay fever, rose fever and other fevers from which they suffer during the pollinating season, many dogs suffer from the same allergies. When the pollen count is high, your dog might suffer, but don't expect him to sneeze and have a runny nose as a human would. Dogs react to pollen allergies the same way they react to fleas—they scratch and bite themselves.

Dogs, like humans, can be tested for allergens. Discuss the testing with your veterinary dermatologist.

AUTO-IMMUNE ILLNESSES
An auto-immune illness is one in which the immune system overacts and does not recognize parts of the affected person; rather, the immune system starts to react as if these parts were foreign and need

THE PROTEIN QUESTION
Your dog's protein needs are changeable. High activity level, stress, climate and other physical factors may require your dog to have more protein in his diet. Check with your veterinarian.

LEG PROBLEMS

The Great Dane is one of the breeds most commonly affected with hypertrophic osteodystrophy, characterized by lameness in the wrist area of the forelegs, accompanied by upper-leg swelling, anorexia, fever, depression and weight loss. This disease primarily affects large-breed dogs at a young age; in the Great Dane, this can be around three months of age. Though the cause is unknown for certain, hypertrophic osteodystrophy may be associated with supplementation of vitamins and/or minerals.

to be destroyed. An example is rheumatoid arthritis, which occurs when the body does not recognize the joints, thus leading to a very painful and damaging reaction in the joints. This has nothing to do with age, so can occur in children. The wear-and-tear arthritis of the older person or dog is osteoarthritis.

Lupus is an auto-immune disease that affects dogs as well as people. It can take variable forms, affecting the kidneys, bones and skin. It can be fatal, so is treated with steroids, which can themselves have very significant side effects. The steroids not only calm down the allergic reaction to the body's tissues, which helps the lupus, but also lessen the body's reaction to real foreign substances such as bacteria, and thin the skin and bones.

FOOD PROBLEMS

FOOD ALLERGIES

Some dogs are allergic to many foods that are best-sellers and highly recommended by breeders and vets. Changing the brand of food that you buy may not eliminate the problem if the element to which the dog is allergic is contained in the new brand.

Recognizing a food allergy is difficult. Humans vomit or have rashes when they eat a food to which they are allergic. Dogs neither vomit nor (usually) develop a rash. They react in the same manner as they do to an airborne or flea allergy; they itch, scratch and bite, thus making the diagnosis extremely difficult. While pollen allergies and parasite bites are usually seasonal, food allergies are year-round problems.

FOOD INTOLERANCE

Food intolerance is the inability of the dog to completely digest certain foods. For instance, puppies that may have done very well on their mother's milk may not do well on cow's milk. The results of food intolerance may be loose bowels, passing gas and stomach pains. These are the only obvious symptoms of food intolerance, which makes diagnosis difficult.

TREATING FOOD PROBLEMS

It is possible to handle food allergies and food intolerance yourself.

Put your dog on a diet that he has never had. Obviously, if he has never eaten this new food, he can't yet have been allergic or intolerant of it. Start with a single ingredient that is not in the dog's diet at the present time. Ingredients like chopped beef or chicken are common in dogs' diets, so try another source of protein like fish or rabbit, or even something more exotic like pheasant. Keep the dog on this diet (with no additives) for a month. If the symptoms of food allergy or intolerance disappear, chances are your dog has a food allergy.

Don't think that the single ingredient cured the problem. You still must find a suitable diet and ascertain which ingredient in the old diet was objectionable. This is most easily done by adding ingredients to the new diet one at a time. Let the dog stay on the modified diet for a month before you add another ingredient. Eventually, you will determine the ingredient that caused the adverse reaction.

An alternative method is to carefully study the ingredients in the diet to which your dog is allergic or intolerant. Identify the main ingredient in this diet and eliminate the main ingredient by buying a different food that does not have that ingredient. Keep experimenting until the symptoms disappear after one month on the new diet.

DETECTING BLOAT
Precautions against bloat/gastric torsion have been previously mentioned, but it is also of utmost important to recognize the symptoms, as studies show the Great Dane to be one the breeds most commonly affected by bloat. It is necessary for your Dane to get immediate veterinary attention if you notice any of the following:

• Your dog's stomach starts to distend, ending up large and as tight as a football;
• Your dog is dribbling, as no saliva can be swallowed;
• Your dog makes frequent attempts to vomit but cannot bring anything up due to the stomach's being closed off;
• Your dog is distressed from pain;
• Your dog starts to suffer from clinical shock, meaning that there is not enough blood in the dog's circulation as the hard, dilated stomach stops the blood from returning to the heart to be pumped around the body. Clinical shock is indicated by pale gums and tongue, as they have been starved of blood. The shocked dog also has glazed, staring eyes.

You have minutes, yes, *minutes*, to get your dog into surgery. If you see any of these symptoms at any time of the day or night, get to the vet immediately. Someone will have to phone and warn that you are on your way (which is a justification for the invention of the cellular phone!) so that they can be prepared to get your pet on the operating table right away.

A male dog flea, *Ctenocephalides canis.*

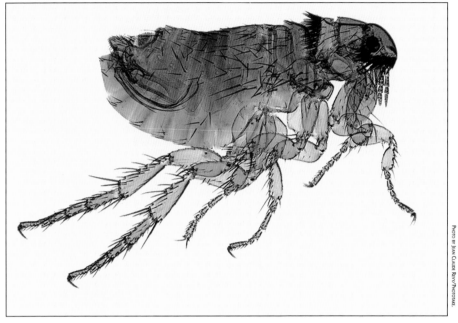

PHOTO BY JEAN CLAUDE REVY/PHOTOTAKE.

EXTERNAL PARASITES

FLEAS

Of all the problems to which dogs are prone, none is more well known and frustrating than fleas. Flea infestation is relatively simple to cure but difficult to prevent. Parasites that are harbored inside the body are a bit more difficult to eradicate but they are easier to control.

To control flea infestation, you have to understand the flea's life cycle. Fleas are often thought of as a summertime problem, but centrally heated homes have changed the patterns and fleas can be found at any time of the year. The most effective method of flea control is a two-stage approach: one stage to kill the adult fleas, and the other to control the development of pre-adult fleas. Unfortunately, no single active ingredient is effective against all stages of the life cycle.

FLEA KILLER CAUTION— "POISON"

Flea-killers are poisonous. You should not spray these toxic chemicals on areas of a dog's body that he licks, including his genitals and his face. Flea killers taken internally are a better answer, but check with your vet in case internal therapy is not advised for your dog.

LIFE CYCLE STAGES

During its life, a flea will pass through four life stages: egg, larva, pupa (or nymph) and adult. The adult stage is the most visible and irritating stage of the flea life cycle, and this is why the majority of flea-control products concentrate on this stage. The fact is that adult fleas account for only 1% of the total flea population, and the other 99% exist in pre-adult stages, i.e., eggs, larvae and nymphs. The pre-adult stages are barely visible to the naked eye.

THE LIFE CYCLE OF THE FLEA

Eggs are laid on the dog, usually in quantities of about 20 or 30, several times a day. The adult female flea must have a blood meal before each egg-laying session. When first laid, the eggs will cling to the dog's hair, as the eggs are still moist. However, they will quickly dry out and fall from the dog, especially if the dog moves around or scratches. Many eggs will fall off in the dog's favorite area or an area in which he spends a lot of time, such as his bed.

Once the eggs fall from the dog onto the carpet or furniture, they will hatch into larvae. This takes from one to ten days. Larvae are not particularly mobile and will usually travel only a few inches from where they hatch. However, they do have a tendency to move away from bright light and heavy

EN GARDE:
CATCHING FLEAS OFF GUARD!
Consider the following ways to arm yourself against fleas:
• Add a small amount of pennyroyal or eucalyptus oil to your dog's bath. These natural remedies repel fleas.
• Supplement your dog's food with fresh garlic (minced or grated) and an hearty amount of brewer's yeast, both of which ward off fleas.
• Use a flea comb on your dog daily. Submerge fleas in a cup of bleach to kill them quickly.
• Confine the dog to only a few rooms to limit the spread of fleas in the home.
• Vacuum daily...and get all of the crevices! Dispose of the bag every few days until the problem is under control.
• Wash your dog's bedding daily. Cover cushions where your dog sleeps with towels, and wash the towels often.

traffic—under furniture and behind doors are common places to find high quantities of flea larvae.

The flea larvae feed on dead organic matter, including adult flea feces, until they are ready to change into adult fleas. Fleas will usually remain as larvae for around seven days. After this period, the larvae will pupate into protective pupae. While inside the pupae, the larvae will undergo

Fleas have been measured as being able to jump 300,000 times and can jump 150 times their length in any direction, including straight up.

metamorphosis and change into adult fleas. This can take as little time as a few days, but the adult fleas can remain inside the pupae waiting to hatch for up to two years. The pupae are signaled to hatch by certain stimuli, such as physical pressure—the pupae's being stepped on, heat from an animal's lying on the pupae or increased carbon-dioxide levels and vibrations—indicating that a suitable host is available.

Once hatched, the adult flea must feed within a few days. Once the adult flea finds a host, it will not leave voluntarily. It only becomes dislodged by grooming or the host animal's scratching.

PHOTO BY DWIGHT R. KUHN.

The adult flea will remain on the host for the duration of its life unless forcibly removed.

TREATING THE ENVIRONMENT AND THE DOG

Treating fleas should be a two-pronged attack. First, the environment needs to be treated; this includes carpets and furniture, especially the dog's bedding and areas underneath furniture. The environment should be treated with a household spray containing an Insect Growth Regulator (IGR) and an insecticide to kill the adult fleas. Most IGRs are effective against eggs and larvae; they actually mimic the fleas' own hormones and stop the eggs and larvae from developing into adult fleas. There are currently no treatments available to attack the pupa stage of the life cycle, so the adult insecticide is used to kill the newly hatched adult fleas before they find a host. Most IGRs are active for many

A scanning electron micrograph of a dog or cat flea, *Ctenocephalides*, magnified more than 100x. This image has been colorized for effect.

S. E. M. BY DR DENNIS KUNKEL, UNIVERSITY OF HAWAII.

THE LIFE CYCLE OF THE FLEA

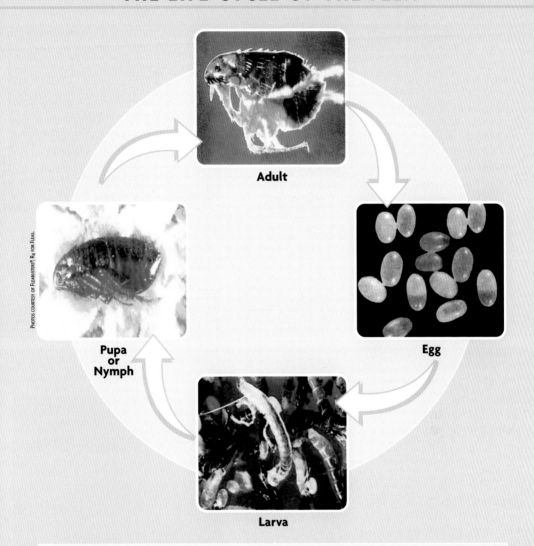

Adult

Pupa or Nymph

Egg

Larva

A LOOK AT FLEAS

Fleas have been around for millions of years and have adapted to changing host animals. They are able to go through a complete life cycle in less than one month or they can extend their lives to almost two years by remaining as pupae or cocoons. They do not need blood or any other food for up to 20 months.

INSECT GROWTH REGULATOR (IGR)

Two types of products should be used when treating fleas—a product to treat the pet and a product to treat the home. Adult fleas represent less than 1% of the flea population. The pre-adult fleas (eggs, larvae and pupae) represent more than 99% of the flea population and are found in the environment; it is in the case of pre-adult fleas that products containing an Insect Growth Regulator (IGR) should be used in the home.

IGRs are a new class of compounds used to prevent the development of insects. They do not kill the insect outright, but instead use the insect's biology against it to stop it from completing its growth. Products that contain methoprene are the world's first and leading IGRs. Used to control fleas and other insects, this type of IGR will stop flea larvae from developing and protect the house for up to seven months.

The American dog tick, *Dermacentor variabilis*, is probably the most common tick found on dogs. Look at the strength in its eight legs! No wonder it's hard to detach them.

The second stage of treatment is to apply an adult insecticide to the dog. Traditionally, this would be in the form of a collar or a spray, but more recent innovations include digestible insecticides that poison the fleas when they ingest the dog's blood. Alternatively, there are drops that, when placed on the back of the dog's neck, spread throughout the dog's hair and skin to kill adult fleas.

TICKS

Though not as common as fleas, ticks are found all over the tropical and temperate world. They don't bite, like fleas; they harpoon. They dig their sharp proboscis (nose) into the dog's skin and drink the blood. Their months, while adult insecticides are only active for a few days.

When treating with a household spray, it is a good idea to vacuum before applying the product. This stimulates as many pupae as possible to hatch into adult fleas. The vacuum cleaner should also be treated with an insecticide to prevent the eggs and larvae that have been collected in the vacuum bag from hatching.

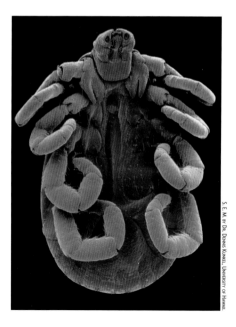

only food and drink is dog's blood. Dogs can get Lyme disease, Rocky Mountain spotted fever, tick bite paralysis and many other diseases from ticks. They may live where fleas are found and they like to hide in cracks or seams in walls. They are controlled the same way fleas are controlled.

The American dog tick, *Dermacentor variabilis*, may well be the most common dog tick in many geographical areas, especially those areas where the climate is hot and humid. Most dog ticks have life expectancies of a week to six months, depending upon climatic conditions. They can neither jump nor fly, but they can crawl slowly and can range up to 16 feet to reach a sleeping or unsuspecting dog.

MITES

Just as fleas and ticks can be problematic for your dog, mites can also lead to an itchy nuisance. Microscopic in size, mites are related to ticks and generally take up permanent residence on their host animal—in this case, your dog! The term *mange* refers to any infestation caused by one of the mighty mites, of which there are six varieties that concern dog owners.

Demodex mites cause a condition known as demodicosis (sometimes called red mange or follicular mange). In normal

DEER-TICK CROSSING

The great outdoors may be fun for your dog, but it also is an home to dangerous ticks. Deer ticks carry a bacterium known as *Borrelia burgdorferi* and are most active in the autumn and spring. When infections are caught early, penicillin and tetracycline are effective antibiotics, but, if left untreated, the bacteria may cause neurological, kidney and cardiac problems as well as long-term trouble with walking and painful joints.

S. E. M. BY DR. ANDREW SPIELMAN/PHOTOTAKE.

PHOTO BY DR. DENNIS KUNKEL, UNIVERSITY OF HAWAII.

The head of an American dog tick, *Dermacentor variabilis*, enlarged and colorized for effect.

The mange mite, *Psoroptes bovis*, can infest cattle and other domestic animals.

Photo by James Hayden/Yoav/Phototake.

Human lice look like dog lice; the two are closely related.

Photo by Dwight R. Kuhn.

dogs, small numbers of these mites live on the hair and skin. In others, the mites increase in number and cause mange. This type of mange is commonly passed from the dam to her puppies and usually shows up on the puppies' muzzles, though demodicosis is not transferable from one normal dog to another. Most dogs recover from this type of mange without any treatment, though topical therapies are commonly prescribed by the vet.

The *Cheyletiellosis* mite is the hook-mouthed culprit associated with "walking dandruff," a condition that affects dogs as well as cats and rabbits. This mite lives on the surface of the animal's skin and is readily transferable through direct or indirect contact with an affected animal. The dandruff is present in the form of scaly skin, which may or may not be itchy. If not treated, this mange can affect a whole kennel of dogs and can be spread to humans as well.

The *Sarcoptes* mite causes intense itching on the dog in the form of a condition known as scabies or sarcoptic mange. The cycle of the *Sarcoptes* mite lasts about three weeks, and the mites live in the top layer of the dog's skin (epidermis), preferably in areas with little hair. Scabies is highly contagious and can be passed to humans. Sometimes an allergic reaction to the mite worsens the severe itching associated with sarcoptic mange.

Ear mites, *Otodectes cynotis,* lead to otodectic mange, which most commonly affects the outer ear canal of the dog, though other areas can be affected as well. Dogs with ear-mite infestation commonly scratch at their ears, causing further irritation, and shake their heads. Dark brown droppings in the outer ear confirm the diagnosis. Your vet can prescribe a treatment to flush out the ears and kill any eggs in the ears. A complete month of treatment is necessary to cure the mange.

Two other mites, less common in dogs, include *Dermanyssus gallinae* (the poultry or red mite) and *Eutrombicula alfreddugesi* (the North American mite associated with trombiculidiasis or chigger infestation). The poultry mite frequently lives on chickens, but can transfer to dogs who spend time near farm animals. Chigger infestation affects dogs in the

DO NOT MIX
Never mix parasite-control products without first consulting your vet. Some products can become toxic when combined with others and can cause fatal consequences.

NOT A DROP TO DRINK
Never allow your dog to swim in polluted water or public areas where water quality can be suspect. Even perfectly clear water can harbor parasites, many of which can cause serious to fatal illnesses in canines. Areas inhabited by water-fowl and other wildlife are especially dangerous.

central US who have exposure to woodlands. The types of mange caused by both of these mites are treatable by veterinarians.

INTERNAL PARASITES
Most animals—fishes, birds and mammals, including dogs and humans—have worms and other parasites that live inside their bodies. According to Dr. Herbert R. Axelrod, the fish pathologist, there are two kinds of parasites: dumb and smart. The smart parasites live in peaceful cooperation with their hosts (symbiosis), while the dumb parasites kill their hosts. Most worm infections are relatively easy to control. If they are not controlled, they weaken the host dog to the point that other medical problems occur, but they do not kill the host as dumb parasites would.

A brown dog tick, *Rhipicephalus sanguineus*, is an uncommon but annoying tick found on dogs.
Photo by Carolina Biological Supply/Phototake.

Photo by Carolina Biological Supply/Phototake.

Above: The roundworm *Rhabditis* can infect both dogs and humans.

Below: The roundworm, *Ascaris lumbricoides.*

ROUNDWORMS

Average-size dogs can pass 1,360,000 roundworm eggs every day. For example, if there were only 1 million dogs in the world, the world would be saturated with thousands of tons of dog feces. These feces would contain around 15,000,000,000 roundworm eggs.

Up to 31% of home yards and children's sand boxes in the US contain roundworm eggs.

Flushing dog's feces down the toilet is not a safe practice because the usual sewage treatments do not destroy roundworm eggs.

Infected puppies start shedding roundworm eggs at three weeks of age. They can be infected by their mother's milk.

Photo by Dwight R. Kuhn.

ROUNDWORMS

The roundworms that infect dogs are known scientifically as *Toxocara canis.* They live in the dog's intestines and shed eggs continually. It has been estimated that a dog produces about 6 or more ounces of feces every day. Each ounce of feces averages hundreds of thousands of roundworm eggs. There are no known areas in which dogs roam that do not contain roundworm eggs. The greatest danger of roundworms is that they infect people, too! It is wise to have your dog tested regularly for roundworms.

In young puppies, roundworms cause bloated bellies, diarrhea, coughing and vomiting, and are transmitted from the dam (through blood or milk). Affected puppies will not appear as animated as normal puppies. The worms appear spaghetti-like, measuring as long as 6 inches. Adult dogs can acquire roundworms through coprophagia (eating contaminated feces) or by killing rodents that carry roundworms.

Roundworm infection can kill puppies and cause severe problems in adults, as the hatched larvae travel to the lungs and trachea through the bloodstream. Cleanliness is the best preventative for roundworms. Always pick up after your dog and dispose of feces in appropriate receptacles.

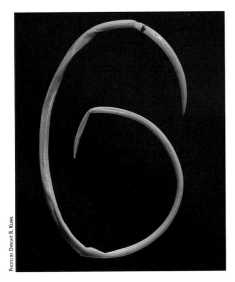

PHOTO BY DWIGHT R. KUHN.

HOOKWORMS

In the United States, dog owners have to be concerned about four different species of hookworm, the most common and most serious of which is *Ancylostoma caninum,* which prefers warm climates. The others are *Ancylostoma braziliense, Ancylostoma tubaeforme* and *Uncinaria stenocephala,* the latter of which is a concern to dogs living in the northern US and Canada, as this species prefers cold climates. Hookworms are dangerous to humans as well as to dogs and cats, and can be the cause of severe anemia due to iron deficiency. The worm uses its teeth to attach itself to the dog's intestines and changes the site of its attachment about six times per day. Each time the worm repositions itself, the dog loses blood and can become anemic. *Ancylostoma caninum* is the most likely of the four species to cause anemia in the dog.

Symptoms of hookworm infection include dark stools, weight loss, general weakness, pale coloration and anemia, as well as possible skin problems. Fortunately, hookworms are easily purged from the affected dog with a number of medications that have proven effective. Discuss these with your veterinarian. Most heartworm preventatives include a hookworm insecticide as well.

Owners also must be aware that hookworms can infect humans, who can acquire the larvae through exposure to contaminated feces. Since the worms cannot complete their life cycle on a human, the worms simply infest the skin and cause irritation. This condition is known as cutaneous larva migrans syndrome. As a preventative, use disposable gloves or a "poop-scoop" to pick up your dog's droppings and prevent your dog (or neighborhood cats) from defecating in children's play areas.

The hookworm *Ancylostoma caninum.*

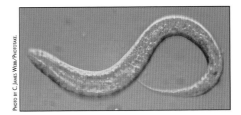

PHOTO BY C. JAMES WEBB/PHOTOTAKE.

The infective stage of the hookworm larva.

TAPEWORMS

Humans, rats, squirrels, foxes, coyotes, wolves and domestic dogs are all susceptible to tapeworm infection. Except in humans, tapeworms are usually not a fatal infection. Infected individuals can harbor 1000 parasitic worms.

Tapeworms, like some other types of worm, are hermaphroditic, meaning male and female in the same worm.

If dogs eat infected rats or mice, or anything else injected with tapeworm, they get the tapeworm disease. One month after attaching to a dog's intestine, the worm starts shedding eggs. These eggs are infective immediately. Infective eggs can live for a few months without a host animal.

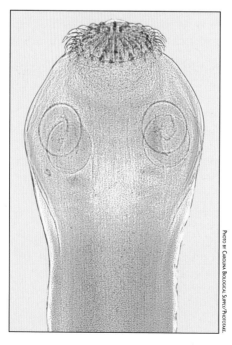

The head and rostellum (the round prominence on the scolex) of a tapeworm, which infects dogs and humans.

Photo by Carolina Biological Supply/Phototake.

TAPEWORMS

There are many species of tapeworm, all of which are carried by fleas! The most common tapeworm affecting dogs is known as *Dipylidium caninum*. The dog eats the flea and starts the tapeworm cycle. Humans can also be infected with tapeworms—so don't eat fleas! Fleas are so small that your dog could pass them onto your hands, your plate or your food and thus make it possible for you to ingest a flea that is carrying tapeworm eggs.

While tapeworm infection is not life-threatening in dogs (smart parasite!), it can be the cause of a very serious liver disease for humans. About 50% of the humans infected with *Echinococcus multilocularis*, a type of tapeworm that causes alveolar hydatid, perish.

WHIPWORMS

In North America, whipworms are counted among the most common parasitic worms in dogs. The whipworm's scientific name is *Trichuris vulpis*. These worms attach themselves in the lower parts of the intestine, where they feed. Affected dogs may only experience upset tummies, colic and diarrhea. These worms, however, can live for months or years in the dog, beginning their larval stage in the small intestine, spending their adult stage in the large intestine and finally passing infective eggs through the dog's feces. The only way to detect whipworms is through a fecal examination, though this is not always foolproof. Treatment for whipworms is tricky, due to the worms' unusual life-cycle pattern, and very often dogs are reinfected due to exposure to infective eggs on the ground. The whipworm eggs can survive in the environment for as long as five years, thus cleaning up droppings in your own backyard as well as in public places is absolutely essential for sanitation purposes and the health of your dog (and other dogs).

THREADWORMS

Though less common than round-worms, hookworms and the other worms mentioned thus far, thread-worms concern dog owners in the southwestern US and Gulf Coast area, where the climate is hot and humid. Living in the small intes-tine of the dog, this worm measures a mere 2 millimeters and is round in shape. Like that of the whip-worm, the threadworm's life cycle is very complex and the eggs and larvae are passed through the feces. A deadly disease in humans, *Strongyloides* readily infects people, and the handling of feces is the most common means of transmission. Threadworms are most often seen in young puppies; bloody diarrhea and pneumonia are symptoms. Sick puppies must be isolated and treated immediately; vets recommend a follow-up treatment one month later.

HEARTWORM PREVENTATIVES

There are many heartworm preventatives on the market, many of which are sold at your veterinarian's office. These products can be given daily or monthly, depending on the manufacturer's instructions. All of these preventatives contain chemical insecticides directed at killing heartworms, which leads to some controversy among dog owners. In effect, heartworm preventatives are necessary evils, though you should determine how necessary based on your pet's lifestyle. There is no doubt that heartworm is a dreadful disease that threatens the life of dogs. However, the likelihood of your dog's being bitten by an infected mosquito is slim in most places, and a mosquito-repellent (or an herbal remedy such as Wormwood or Black Walnut) is much safer for your dog and will not compromise his immune system (the way heartworm preventatives will). Should you decide to use the traditional preventative "medications," you can consider giving the pill every other or third month. Since the toxins in the pill will kill the heartworms at all stages of development, the pill would be effective in killing larvae, nymphs or adults and it takes four months for the larvae to reach the adult stage. Thus, there is no rationale to poisoning the dog's system on a monthly basis. Lastly, do not give the pill during the winter months since there are no mosquitoes around to pass on their infection, unless you live in a tropical environment.

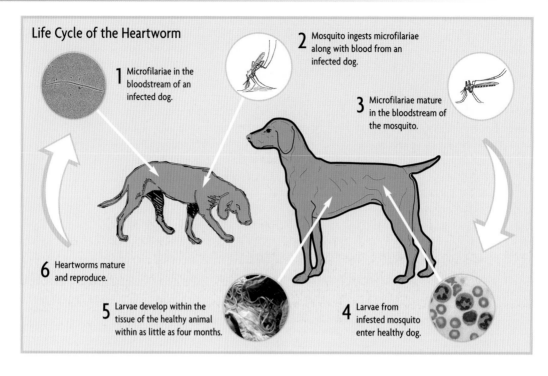

Life Cycle of the Heartworm

1 Microfilariae in the bloodstream of an infected dog.

2 Mosquito ingests microfilariae along with blood from an infected dog.

3 Microfilariae mature in the bloodstream of the mosquito.

4 Larvae from infested mosquito enter healthy dog.

5 Larvae develop within the tissue of the healthy animal within as little as four months.

6 Heartworms mature and reproduce.

HEARTWORMS

Heartworms are thin, extended worms up to 12 inches long, which live in a dog's heart and the major blood vessels surrounding it. Dogs may have up to 200 worms. Symptoms may be loss of energy, loss of appetite, coughing, the development of a pot belly and anemia.

Heartworms are transmitted by mosquitoes. The mosquito drinks the blood of an infected dog and takes in larvae with the blood. The larvae, called microfilariae, develop within the body of the mosquito and are passed on to the next dog bitten after the larvae mature. It takes two to three weeks for the larvae to develop to the infective stage within the body of the mosquito. Dogs are usually treated at about six weeks of age and maintained on a prophylactic dose given monthly.

Blood testing for heartworms is not necessarily indicative of how seriously your dog is infected. Although this is a dangerous disease, it is not easy for a dog to be infected. Discuss the various preventatives with your vet, as there are many different types now available. Together you can decide on a safe course of prevention for your dog.

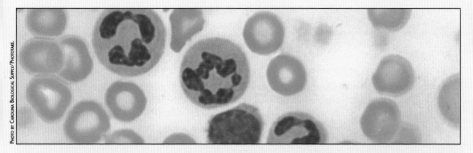

Magnified heart-worm larvae, *Dirofilaria immitis.*

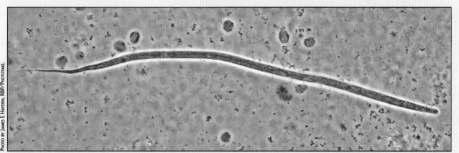

Heartworm, *Dirofilaria immitis.*

The heart of a dog infected with canine heart-worm, *Dirofilaria immitis.*

HOMEOPATHY:
an alternative
to conventional
medicine

"Less is Most"

Using this principle, the strength of a homeopathic remedy is measured by the number of serial dilutions that were undertaken to create it. The greater the number of serial dilutions, the greater the strength of the homeopathic remedy. The potency of a remedy that has been made by making a dilution of 1 part in 100 parts (or 1/100) is 1c or 1cH. If this remedy is subjected to a series of further dilutions, each one being 1/100, a more dilute and stronger remedy is produced. If the remedy is diluted in this way six times, it is called 6c or 6cH. A dilution of 6c is 1 part in 1,000,000,000,000. In general, higher potencies in more frequent doses are better for acute symptoms and lower potencies in more infrequent doses are more useful for chronic, long-standing problems.

CURING OUR DOGS NATURALLY

Holistic medicine means treating the whole animal as a unique, perfect living being. Generally, holistic treatments do not suppress the symptoms that the body naturally produces, as do most medications prescribed by conventional doctors and vets. Holistic methods seek to cure disease by regaining balance and harmony in the patient's environment. Some of these methods include use of nutritional therapy, herbs, flower essences, aromatherapy, acupuncture, massage, chiropractic and, of course, the most popular holistic approach, homeopathy.

Homeopathy is a theory or system of treating illness with small doses of substances which, if administered in larger quantities, would produce the symptoms that the patient already has. This approach is often described as "like cures like." Although modern veterinary medicine is geared toward the "quick fix," homeopathy relies on the belief that, given the time, the body is able to heal itself and return to its natural, healthy state.

Choosing a remedy to cure a problem in our dogs is the difficult part of homeopathy. Consult with your vet for a professional diagnosis of your dog's symptoms. Often these symptoms require

immediate conventional care. If your vet is willing and knowledgeable, you may attempt a homeopathic remedy. Be aware that cortisone prevents homeopathic remedies from working. There are hundreds of possibilities and combinations to cure many problems in dogs, from basic physical problems such as excessive shedding, fleas or other parasites, unattractive doggy odor, bad breath, upset tummy, obesity, dry, oily or dull coat, diarrhea, ear problems or eye discharge (including tears and dry or mucousy matter), to behavioral abnormalities such as fear of loud noises, habitual licking, poor appetite, excessive barking and various phobias. From alumina to zincum metallicum, the remedies span the planet and the imagination…from flowers and weeds to chemicals, insect droppings, diesel smoke and volcanic ash.

Using "Like to Treat Like"

Unlike conventional medicines that suppress symptoms, homeopathic remedies treat illnesses with small doses of substances that, if administered in larger quantities, would produce the symptoms that the patient already has. While the same homeopathic remedy can be used to treat different symptoms in different dogs, here are some interesting remedies and their uses.

Apis Mellifica
(made from honey bee venom) can be used for allergies or to reduce swelling that occurs in acutely infected kidneys.

Calcarea Fluorica
(made from calcium fluoride, which helps harden bone structure) can be useful in treating hard lumps in tissues.

Diesel Smoke
can be used to help control travel sickness.

Natrum Muriaticum
(made from common salt, sodium chloride) is useful in treating thin, thirsty dogs.

Nitricum Acidum
(made from nitric acid) is used for symptoms you would expect to see from contact with acids such as lesions, especially where the skin joins the linings of body orifices or openings such as the lips and nostrils.

Symphytum
(made from the herb Knitbone, *Symphytum officianale*) is used to encourage bones to heal.

Urtica Urens
(made from the common stinging nettle) is used in treating painful, irritating rashes.

Number-One Killer Disease in Dogs: CANCER

In every age, there is a word associated with a disease or plague that causes humans to shudder. In the 21st century, that word is "cancer." Just as cancer is the leading cause of death in humans, it claims nearly half the lives of dogs that die from a natural disease as well as half the dogs that die over the age of ten years.

Described as a genetic disease, cancer becomes a greater risk as the dog ages. Vets and dog owners have become increasingly aware of the threat of cancer to dogs. Statistics reveal that one dog in every five will develop cancer, the most common of which is skin cancer. Many cancers, including prostate, ovarian and breast cancer, can be avoided by spaying and neutering our dogs by the age of six months.

Early detection of cancer can save or extend a dog's life, so it is absolutely vital for owners to have their dogs examined by a qualified vet or oncologist immediately upon detection of any abnormality. Certain dietary guidelines have also proven to reduce the onset and spread of cancer. Foods based on fish rather than beef, due to the presence of Omega-3 fatty acids, are recommended. Other amino acids such as glutamine have significant benefits for canines, particularly those breeds that show a greater susceptibility to cancer.

Cancer management and treatments promise hope for future generations of canines. Since the disease is genetic, breeders should never breed a dog whose parents, grandparents and any related siblings have developed cancer. It is difficult to know whether to exclude an otherwise healthy dog from a breeding program as the disease does not manifest itself until the dog's senior years.

RECOGNIZE CANCER WARNING SIGNS

Since early detection can possibly rescue your dog from becoming a cancer statistic, it is essential for owners to recognize the possible signs and seek the assistance of a qualified professional.

- Abnormal bumps or lumps that continue to grow
- Bleeding or discharge from any body cavity
- Persistent stiffness or lameness
- Recurrent sores or sores that do not heal
- Inappetence
- Breathing difficulties
- Weight loss
- Bad breath or odors
- General malaise and fatigue
- Eating and swallowing problems
- Difficulty urinating and defecating

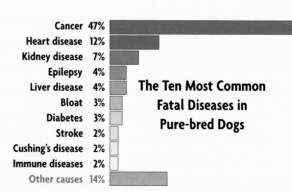

Cancer	47%
Heart disease	12%
Kidney disease	7%
Epilepsy	4%
Liver disease	4%
Bloat	3%
Diabetes	3%
Stroke	2%
Cushing's disease	2%
Immune diseases	2%
Other causes	14%

The Ten Most Common Fatal Diseases in Pure-bred Dogs

YOUR SENIOR
GREAT DANE

The term *old* is a qualitative term. For dogs, as well as their masters, old is relative. Certainly we can all distinguish between a puppy Great Dane and an adult Great Dane—there are the obvious physical traits, such as size, appearance and facial expressions, as well as personality traits. Puppies and young dogs like to play with children. Children's natural exuberance is a good match for the seemingly endless energy of young dogs. They like to run, jump, chase and retrieve. When dogs grow up and cease their interaction with children, they are often thought of as being too old to play with the kids. On the other hand, if a Great Dane is only exposed to people with quieter lifestyles, his life will normally be less active and the changes in his activity level as he ages will not be as obvious.

If people live to be 100 years old, dogs live to be 20 years old. While this is a good rule of thumb, it is very inaccurate, especially with the Great Dane. When trying to compare dog years to human years, you cannot make a generalization about all dogs. You can make the general-ization that eight to ten years is a good lifespan for a Great Dane, which is lower than average for most breeds. Great Danes (and large breeds in general) do not live as long as smaller pure-bred

SENIOR SIGNS
An old dog starts to show one or more of the following symptoms:
- The hair on the face and paws starts to turn gray. The color breakdown usually starts around the eyes and mouth.
- Sleep patterns are deeper and longer, and the old dog is harder to awaken.
- Food intake diminishes.
- Responses to calls, whistles and other signals are ignored more and more.
- Eye contact does not evoke tail wagging (assuming it once did).

dogs, which may live to 12 or 15 years of age.

Dogs are generally considered mature within three years (or earlier), but they can reproduce before reaching full maturity. So the first three years of a dog's life are like seven times that of comparable humans. Again to generalize, that means a 3-year-old dog is like a 21-year-old human. However, as the curve of comparison shows, there is no hard and fast rule for comparing dog and human ages. The comparison is made even more difficult, for not all humans age at the same rate...and human females live longer than human males.

WHAT TO LOOK FOR IN SENIORS

Most vets and behaviorists use the seven-year mark as the time to consider a dog a *senior*. This term does not imply that the dog is geriatric and has begun to fail in mind and body. Aging is essentially a slowing process. Humans readily admit that they feel a difference in their activity level from age 20 to 30, and then from 30 to 40, etc. By treating the seven-year-old dog as

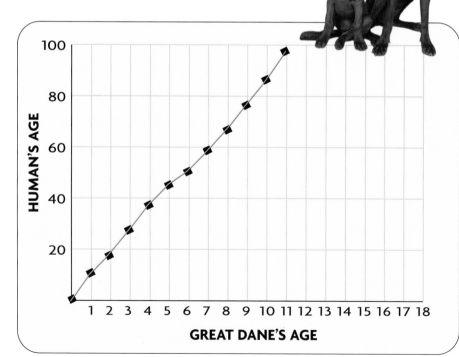

a senior, owners are able to implement certain therapeutic and preventative medical strategies with the help of their vets. A senior-care program should include at least two veterinary visits per year and screening sessions to determine the dog's health status, as well as nutritional counseling. Vets determine the senior dog's health status through a blood smear for a complete blood count, serum chemistry profile with electrolytes, urinalysis, blood pres-

A little gray on the muzzle doesn't keep the Great Dane from looking distinguished and regal in his senior years.

sure check, electrocardiogram, ocular tonometry (pressure on the eyeball) and dental prophylaxis.

Such an extensive program for senior dogs is well advised before owners start to see the obvious physical signs of aging, such as slower and inhibited movement, graying, increased sleep/nap periods and disinterest in play and other activity. This preventative program could mean a longer, healthier life for the aging dog. Among the physical problems common in aging dogs are the loss of sight and hearing, arthritis, kidney and liver failure, diabetes mellitus, heart disease and Cushing's disease (a hormonal disease).

In addition to the physical manifestations discussed, there are some behavioral changes and problems related to aging dogs. Dogs suffering from hearing or vision loss, dental discomfort or

NOTICING THE SYMPTOMS

The symptoms listed below are symptoms that gradually appear and become more noticeable. They are not life-threatening; however, the symptoms below are to be taken very seriously and warrant a discussion with your veterinarian:

- Your dog cries and whimpers when he moves, and he stops running completely.
- Convulsions start or become more serious and frequent. The usual convulsion (spasm) is when the dog stiffens and starts to tremble, being unable or unwilling to move. The seizure usually lasts for 5 to 30 minutes.
- Your dog drinks more water and urinates more frequently. Wetting and bowel accidents take place indoors without warning.
- Vomiting becomes more and more frequent.

arthritis can become aggressive. Likewise, the near-deaf and/or blind dog may be startled more easily and react in an unexpectedly aggressive manner. Seniors suffering from senility can become more impatient and irritable. Housesoiling accidents are associated with loss of mobility, kidney problems and loss of sphincter control as well as plaque accumulation, physiological brain changes and reactions to medications. Older dogs, just like young puppies, can suffer from

Gray hair is a sign of old age in dogs just as it is in humans...on dogs, the hair on the face usually turns gray first.

> **AGING ADDITIVES**
> A healthy diet is important for dogs of all ages, but older dogs may benefit from the addition of supplements like antioxidants, which fight the aging process, and vitamin B, which aids the kidneys. Check with your vet before adding these or any supplements to your pet's diet.

separation anxiety, which can lead to excessive barking, whining, housesoiling and destructive behavior. Seniors may become

fearful of everyday sounds such as vacuum cleaners, heaters, thunder and passing traffic. Some dogs have difficulty sleeping due to discomfort, the need for frequent potty visits and the like.

Owners should avoid spoiling the older dog with too many fatty treats. Obesity is a common problem in older dogs and subtracts years from their lives. Keep the senior dog as trim as possible since excessive weight puts additional stress on the body's vital organs. Some breeders recommend supplementing the diet with foods high in fiber and lower in calories. Adding fresh vegetables and marrow broth to the senior's diet makes a tasty, low-calorie, low-fat supplement. Vets also offer specialty diets for senior dogs that are worth exploring.

Your dog, as he nears his twilight years, needs his owner's patience and good care more than ever. Never punish an older dog for an accident or abnormal behavior. For all the years of love, protection and companionship that your dog has provided, he deserves special attention and courtesies. The older dog may need to relieve himself at 3 a.m. because he can no longer hold it for eight hours. Older dogs may not be able to remain crated for more than two or three hours. It may be time to give up a couch or chair to your old friend.

Although he may not seem as enthusiastic about your attention and petting, he does appreciate the considerations you offer as he gets older.

Your Great Dane does not understand why his world is slowing down. Owners must make the transition into the golden years as pleasant and rewarding as possible.

AN ANCIENT ACHE

As ancient a disease as any, arthritis remains poorly explained for human and dog alike. Fossils dating back 100 million years show the deterioration caused by arthritis. Human fossils two million years old show the disease in man. The most common type of arthritis affecting dogs is known as osteoarthritis, which occurs in adult dogs before their senior years. Obesity aggravating the dog's joints has been cited as a factor in arthritis.

Rheumatoid disease destroys joint cartilage and causes arthritic joints. Pituitary dysfunctions as well as diabetes have been associated with arthritis. Veterinarians treat arthritis variously, including aspirin, "bed rest" in the dog's crate, physical therapy and exercise, heat therapy (with a heating pad), providing soft bedding materials and treatment with corticosteroids (to reduce pain and swelling temporarily). Your vet will be able to recommend a course of action to help relieve your arthritic pal.

Cremation is an option for those who wish to memorialize their deceased pets. Cemeteries usually have areas in which to accommodate urns that contain the dog's ashes.

> **EUTHANASIA**
> Euthanasia must be performed by a licensed veterinarian. There also may be societies for the prevention of cruelty to animals in your area. They often offer this service upon a vet's recommendation.

WHEN THE TIME COMES

You are never fully prepared to make a rational decision about putting your dog to sleep. It is very obvious that you love your Great Dane or you would not be reading this book. Putting a loved dog to sleep is extremely difficult. It is a decision that must be made with your vet. You are usually forced to make the decision when your dog experiences life-threatening symptoms that require you to seek veterinary help.

If the prognosis of the malady indicates the end is near and your beloved pet will only suffer more and experience no enjoyment for the balance of his life, then euthanasia is the right choice.

There are cemeteries for deceased pets. Consult with your vet to help find one in your area.

Owners may choose to memorialize their dog with a marker in their own yard.

WHAT IS EUTHANASIA?

Euthanasia derives from the Greek, meaning *good death.* In other words, it means the planned, painless killing of a dog suffering from a painful, incurable condition, or who is so aged that he cannot walk, see, eat or control his excretory functions.

Euthanasia is usually accomplished by injection with an overdose of an anesthesia or barbiturate. Aside from the prick of the needle, the experience is usually painless.

MAKING THE DECISION

The decision to euthanize your dog is never easy. The days during which the dog becomes ill and the end occurs can be unusually stressful for you. If this is your first experience with the death of a loved one, you may need the comfort dictated by your religious beliefs. If you are the head of the family and have children, you should have involved them in the decision of putting your Great Dane to sleep. Usually your dog can be main-

---

TALK IT OUT

The more openly your family discusses the whole stressful occurrence of the aging and eventual loss of a beloved pet, the easier it will be for you.

TO THE RESCUE

Some people choose to adopt or "rescue" an older dog instead of buying a new puppy. Some older dogs may have come from abusive environments and be fearful, while other dogs may have developed many bad habits; both situations can present challenges to their new owners. Training an older dog will take more time and patience, but persistence and an abundance of praise and love can transform a dog into a well-behaved, loyal companion.

tained on drugs for a few days in order to give you ample time to make a decision. During this time, talking with members of your family or even people who have lived through this same experience can ease the burden of your inevitable decision.

THE FINAL RESTING PLACE

Dogs can have some of the same privileges as humans. Your dog can be buried in a pet cemetery, which is generally expensive, or he can be buried in your yard in a place suitably marked with a stone or newly planted tree or bush. Alternatively, dogs can be cremated and the ashes returned to you, or some people prefer to leave their deceased dogs at the veterinary clinic.

All of these options should be discussed frankly and openly with your vet. Do not be afraid to ask financial questions. For example, cremations can be individual, but a less expensive option is mass cremation, although of course the ashes cannot then be returned. Vets can usually arrange burial or cremation services on your behalf.

GETTING ANOTHER DOG?

The grief of losing your beloved dog will be as lasting as the grief of losing a human friend or relative. In most cases, if your dog died of old age (if there is such a thing), he had slowed down considerably. Do you want a new Great Dane puppy to replace him? Or are you better off in finding a more mature Great Dane, say two to three years of age, which will usually be housebroken and will have an already developed personality. In this case, you can find out if you like each other after a few hours of being together.

The decision is, of course, your own. Do you want another Great Dane or perhaps a different breed so as to avoid comparison with your beloved friend? Most people usually buy the same breed because they know (and love) the characteristics of that breed. Then, too, they often know people who have the same breed and perhaps they are lucky enough that a breeder they know and respect expects a litter soon. What could be better?

SHOWING YOUR
GREAT DANE

When you purchase your Great Dane, you will make it clear to the breeder whether you want one just as a lovable companion and pet, or if you hope to be buying a Great Dane with show prospects. No reputable breeder will sell you a young puppy and tell you that it is *definitely* of show quality, for so much can go wrong during the early months of a puppy's development. If you plan to show, what you will hopefully have acquired is a puppy with "show potential."

To the novice, exhibiting a Great Dane in the show ring may look easy, but it takes a lot of hard work and devotion to do top winning at a show such as the prestigious Westminster Kennel Club dog show, not to mention a little luck too!

The first concept that the canine novice learns when watching a dog show is that each dog first competes against members of its own breed. Once the judge has selected the best member of each breed (Best of Breed), provided that the show is judged on a Group system, that chosen dog will compete with other dogs in its group. Finally, the dogs chosen first in each group will compete for Best in Show.

The second concept that you must understand is that the dogs are not actually compared against one another. The judge compares each dog against its breed standard, the written description of the ideal specimen that is approved by the American Kennel Club (AKC). While some early breed standards were indeed based on specific dogs that were famous or popular, many dedicated enthusiasts say that a perfect specimen, as described in the standard, has never walked into a show ring, has never been bred and, to the woe of dog breeders around the globe, does not exist. Breeders attempt to get as close to this ideal as possible with every litter, but theoretically the "perfect" dog is so elusive that it is impossible. (And if the "perfect" dog were born, breeders and judges would never agree that it was indeed "perfect.")

AKC GROUPS

For showing purposes, the American Kennel Club divides its recognized breeds into seven groups: Working Dogs, Sporting Dogs, Hounds, Terriers, Toys, Non-Sporting Dogs and Herding Dogs.

If you are interested in exploring the world of dog showing, your best bet is to join your local breed club or the national parent club, which is the Great Dane Club of America. These clubs often host both regional and national specialties, shows only for Great Danes, which can include conformation as well as obedience and other performance tests. Even if you have no intention of competing with your Great Dane, a specialty is like a festival for lovers of the breed who congregate to share their favorite topic: Great Danes! Clubs also send out newsletters, and some organize training days and seminars in order that people may learn more about their chosen breed. To locate the breed club closest to you, contact the American Kennel Club, which furnishes the rules and regulations for all of these events plus general dog registration and other basic requirements of dog ownership.

In the US, the American Kennel Club offers three kinds of conformation shows: an all-breed show (for all AKC-recognized breeds); a specialty show (for one breed only, usually sponsored by the parent club); and a Group show (for all breeds in the Group).

For a dog to become an AKC champion of record, the dog must accumulate 15 points at the shows from at least three different judges, including two "majors." A "major"

is defined as a three-, four- or five-point win, and the number of points per win is determined on the number of dogs entered in the show on the day. Depending on the breed, the number of points that are awarded varies. In a popular breed, more dogs are needed to rack up the points. At any dog show, only one dog and one bitch of each breed can win points.

Dog showing does not offer "co-ed" classes. Dogs and bitches never compete against each other in the classes. Non-champion dogs are called "class dogs" because they compete in one of five classes. Dogs are entered in a particular class depending on its age and previous show wins. To begin, there is the Puppy Class (for 6- to 9-month-olds and for 9- to 12-month-olds); this class is followed by the Novice Class (for dogs that have not won any first prizes except in the Puppy Class or three first prizes in the Novice Class and have not accumulated any points toward their champion title); the Bred-by-Exhibitor Class (for dogs handled by their breeders or handled by one of the breeder's immediate family); the American-bred Class (for dogs bred in the USA!); and the Open Class (for any dog that is not a champion).

The judge at the show begins judging the Puppy Class, first dogs and then bitches, and proceeds through the classes. The judge places his winners first through fourth in each class. In the Winners Class, the first-place winners of each class compete with one another to determine Winners Dog and Winners Bitch. The judge also places a Reserve Winners Dog and Reserve Winners Bitch, which could be awarded the points in the case of a disqualification. The Winners Dog and Winners Bitch, the two that are awarded the points for the breed, then compete with any champions of record entered in the show. The judge reviews the Winners Dog, Winners Bitch and all the other champions to select his Best of Breed. The Best of Winners is selected between the Winners Dog and Winners Bitch. Were one of these two to be selected Best of Breed, it would automatically be named Best of Winners as well. Finally the judge selects his Best of Opposite Sex to the Best of Breed winner.

At a Group show or all-breed show, the Best of Breed winners from each breed then compete against one another for Group One through Group Four. The judge compares each Best of Breed to its breed standard, and the dog that most closely lives up to the ideal for its breed is selected as Group One. Finally, all seven group winners (from the Working Group, Toy Group, Hound Group, etc.) compete for Best in Show.

To find out about dog shows in your area, you can subscribe to the American Kennel Club's monthly

CONTACT INFORMATION
You can get information about dog shows from the national kennel clubs:

American Kennel Club
5580 Centerview Dr., Raleigh, NC 27606-3390
www.akc.org

United Kennel Club
100 E. Kilgore Road, Kalamazoo, MI 49002
www.ukcdogs.com

Canadian Kennel Club
89 Skyway Ave., Suite 100, Etobicoke, Ontario
M9W 6R4 Canada
www.ckc.ca

The Kennel Club
1-5 Clarges St., Piccadilly, London W1Y 8AB, UK
www.the-kennel-club.org.uk

magazine, The *American Kennel Gazette* and the accompanying *Events Calendar*. You can also look in your local newspaper for advertisements for dog shows in your area or go on the Internet to the AKC's website, www.akc.org.

If your Great Dane is six months of age or older and registered with the AKC, you can enter him in a dog show where the breed is offered classes. Provided that your Great Dane does not have a disqualifying fault, he can compete. Only unaltered dogs can be entered in a dog show, so if you have spayed or neutered your Great Dane, you cannot compete in conformation shows. The reason for this is simple. Dog shows are the main forum to prove which representatives in a breed are worthy of being bred. Only dogs that have achieved championships—the AKC "seal of approval" for quality of pure-bred dogs—should be bred. Altered dogs, however, can participate in other AKC events such as obedience trials and the Canine Good Citizen program.

Before you actually step into the ring, you would be well advised to sit back and observe the judge's ring procedure. If it is your first time in the ring, do not be over-anxious and run to the front of the line. It is much better to stand back and study how the exhibitor in front of you is performing. The judge asks each handler to "stack" the dog, hopefully showing the dog off to his best advantage. The judge will observe the dog from a distance and from different angles, and approach the dog to check his teeth, overall structure, alertness and muscle tone, as well as consider how well the dog "conforms" to the standard. Most

importantly, the judge will have the exhibitor move the dog around the ring in some pattern that he should specify (another advantage to not going first, but always listen since some judges change their directions—and the judge is always right!). Finally, the judge will give the dog one last look before moving on to the next exhibitor.

If you are not in the top four in your class at your first show, do not be discouraged. Be patient and consistent, and you may eventually find yourself in a winning line-up. Remember that the winners were once in your shoes and have devoted many hours and much money to earn the placement. If you find that your dog is losing every time and never getting a nod, it may be time to consider a different dog sport or just to enjoy your Great Dane as a pet. Parent clubs offer other events, such as agility, tracking, obedience, instinct tests and more, which may be of interest to the owner of a well-trained Great Dane.

OBEDIENCE TRIALS
Obedience trials in the US trace back to the early 1930s, when organized obedience training was developed to demonstrate how well dog and owner could work together. The pioneer of obedience trials is Mrs. Helen Whitehouse Walker, a Standard Poodle fancier, who designed a series of exercises

after the Associated Sheep, Police Army Dog Society of Great Britain. Since the days of Mrs. Walker, obedience trials have grown by leaps and bounds, and today there are over 2,000 trials held in the US every year, with more than 100,000 dogs competing. Any AKC-registered dog can enter an obedience trial, regardless of conformational disqualifications or neutering.

Obedience trials are divided into three levels of progressive difficulty. At the first level, the Novice, dogs compete for the title Companion Dog (CD); at the intermediate level, the Open, dogs compete for the title Companion Dog Excellent (CDX); and at the advanced level, the Utility, dogs compete for the title Utility Dog (UD). Classes are sub-divided into "A" (for beginners) and "B" (for more experienced handlers). A perfect score at any level is 200, and a dog must score 170 or better to earn a "leg," of which three are needed to earn the title. To earn points, the dog must score more than 50% of the available points in each exercise; the possible points range from 20 to 40.

Once a dog has earned the UD title, he can compete with other proven obedience dogs for the coveted title of Utility Dog Excellent (UDX), which requires that the dog win "legs" in ten shows. Utility Dogs who earn "legs" in Open B and Utility B earn points toward

their Obedience Trial Champion titles. To become an OTCh., a dog needs to earn 100 points, which requires three first places in Open B and Utility under three different judges.

The Grand Prix of obedience trials, the AKC National Obedience Invitational gives qualifying Utility Dogs the chance to win the newest and highest title: National Obedience Champion (NOC). Only the top 25 ranked obedience dogs, plus any dog ranked in the top 3 in its breed, are allowed to compete.

AGILITY TRIALS
Having had its origins in the UK back in 1977, agility had its official AKC beginning in the US in August 1994, when the first licensed agility trials were held. The AKC allows all registered breeds (including Miscellaneous Class breeds) to participate, providing the dog is 12 months of age or older. Agility is designed so

Correct movement indicates correct structure, so it's a good way to evaluate the dog's conformation. Breed standards specify the dog's desired movement.

that the handler demonstrates how well the dog can work at his side. The handler directs his dog over an obstacle course that includes jumps as well as tires, the dog walk, weave poles, pipe tunnels, collapsed tunnels, etc. While working his way through the course, the dog must keep one eye and ear on the handler and the rest of his body on the course. The handler gives verbal and hand signals to guide the dog through the course.

The first organization to promote agility trials in the US was the United States Dog Agility Association, Inc. (USDAA), which was established in 1986 and spawned numerous member clubs around the country. Both the USDAA and the AKC offer titles to winning dogs.

Agility is great fun for dog and owner, with many rewards for everyone involved. Interested owners should join a training club that has obstacles and experienced agility handlers who can introduce you and your dog to the "ropes" (and tires, tunnels, etc.).

TRACKING

Any dog is capable of tracking, using his nose to follow a trail. Tracking tests are exciting and competitive ways to test your Great Dane's ability to search and rescue. The AKC started tracking tests in 1937, when the first AKC-licensed test took place as part of the Utility level at an obedience trial. Ten years later in 1947, the AKC offered the first title, Tracking Dog (TD). It was not until 1980 that the AKC added the Tracking Dog Excellent title (TDX), which was followed by the Versatile Surface Tracking title (VST) in 1995. The title Champion Tracker (CT) is awarded to a dog who has earned all three titles.

In the beginning level of tracking, the owner follows the dog through a field on a long lead. To earn the TD title, the dog must follow a track laid by a human 30 to 120 minutes prior. The track is about 500 yards long with up to 5 directional changes. The TDX requires that the dog follow a track that is 3 to 5 hours old over a course up to 1,000 yards long with up to 7 directional changes. The VST requires that the dog follow a track up to five hours old through an urban setting.

Lined up for the judge, these dogs and handlers await their turn for evaluation.

BEHAVIOR OF YOUR
GREAT DANE

As a Great Dane owner, you have selected your dog so that you and your loved ones can have a companion, a protector, a friend and a four-legged family member. You invest time, money and effort to care for and train the family's new charge. Of course, this chosen canine behaves perfectly! Well, perfectly like a *dog*.

THINK LIKE A DOG

Dogs do not think like humans, nor do humans think like dogs, though we try. Unfortunately, a dog is incapable of working out how humans think, so the responsibility falls on the owner to adopt a viable canine mindset. Dogs cannot rationalize, and dogs exist in the present moment. Many a dog owner makes the mistake in training of thinking that he can reprimand his dog for something the dog did a while ago. Basically, you cannot even reprimand a dog for something he did 20 seconds ago! Either catch him in the act or forget it! It is a waste of your and your dog's time—in his mind, you are reprimanding him for whatever he is doing at that moment.

The following behavioral problems represent some that owners most commonly encounter. Every dog is unique and every situation is unique. No author could purport for you to solve your Great Dane's problem simply by reading a chapter in a breed book. Here we outline some basic "dogspeak" so that owners' chances of solving behavioral problems are increased. Discuss bad habits with your vet and he can recommend a behavioral specialist to consult in appropriate cases. Since behavioral abnormalities are the leading reason for owners' abandoning their pets, we hope that you will make a valiant effort to solve your Great Dane's problem. Patience and understanding are virtues that must dwell in every pet-loving household.

AGGRESSION

This is a potential problem that concerns owners of Great Danes. Aggression can be a very big problem in dogs, but more so in a breed with a fighting background, even though today's Great Danes should be gentle and temperamentally sound. Aggression, when not controlled, always becomes dangerous. An aggressive dog, no matter the size, may lunge at, bite or even attack a person or another dog. Aggressive behavior is not to be tolerated. It is more than just inappropriate behavior; it is not safe, especially with a large, powerful breed such as the Great Dane.

It is painful for a family to watch its dog become unpredictable in his behavior to the point where they are afraid of him. While not all aggressive behavior is dangerous, growling, baring teeth, etc., can be frightening. It is important to ascertain why the dog is acting in this manner. Aggression is a display of dominance, and the dog should not have the dominant role in its pack, which is, in this case, your family.

It is important not to challenge an aggressive dog as this could provoke an attack. Observe your Great Dane's body language. Does he make direct eye contact and stare? Does he try to make himself as large as possible: ears pricked, chest out, tail erect? Height and size signify authority in a dog pack—being taller or "above" another dog literally means that he is "above" in the social status, a position well known by the Dane. These body signals tell you that your Great Dane thinks he is in charge, a problem that needs to be addressed. An aggressive dog is unpredictable: you never know when he is going to strike and what he is going to do. You cannot understand why a dog that is playful and loving one minute is growling and snapping the next.

Fear is a common cause of aggression in dogs. It is not always easy, but if you can isolate what brings out the fear reaction, you can help the dog get over it. Supervise your Great Dane's interactions with people and other dogs, and praise the dog when it goes well. If he starts to act aggressively in a situation, correct him and remove him from the situation. Do not let people approach the dog and start petting him without your express permission. That way, you can have the dog sit to accept petting, and praise him when he behaves properly. You are focusing on praise and on modifying his behavior by rewarding him when he acts appropriately. By being gentle and by supervising his interactions, you are showing him that there is no need to be afraid or defensive.

The best solution is to consult a behavioral specialist, one who has experience with the Great Dane if possible. Together, perhaps you can pinpoint the cause of your dog's aggression and do something about it. An aggressive dog cannot be trusted, and a dog that cannot be trusted is not safe to have as a family pet. If, very unusually, you find that your pet has become untrustworthy and you feel it necessary to seek a new home with a more suitable family and environment, explain fully to the new owners all your reasons for rehoming the dog to be fair to all concerned. In the *very* worst case, you will have to consider euthanasia.

AGGRESSION TOWARD OTHER DOGS

In general, a dog's aggressive behavior toward another dog stems from not enough exposure to other dogs at an early age. In Great Danes, early socialization with other dogs is absolutely essential. If other dogs make your Great Dane nervous and agitated, he will lash out as a defense mechanism. A dog who has not received sufficient exposure to other canines tends to believe that he is the only dog on the planet. The animal becomes so dominant that he does not even show signs that he is fearful or threatened. Without growling or any other physical signal as a warning, he will lunge at and bite the other dog.

A way to correct this is to let your Great Dane approach another dog when walking on leash. Watch very closely, and, at the very first sign of aggression, correct your Great Dane and pull him away. Scold him for any sign of discomfort, and then praise him when he ignores or tolerates the other dog. Keep this up until he stops the aggressive behavior, learns to ignore the other dog or accepts other dogs. Praise him lavishly for his correct behavior.

DOMINANT AGGRESSION

A social hierarchy is firmly established in a wild dog pack. The dog

DOGGIE DEMOCRACY
Your dog inherited the pack-leader mentality. He only knows about pecking order. He instinctively wants to be top dog, but you have to convince him that you are boss. There is no such thing as living in a democracy with your dog. You are the one who must always make the rules.

wants to dominate those under him and please those above him. Dogs know that there must be a leader. If you are not the obvious choice for emperor, the dog will assume the throne! These conflicting innate desires are what a dog owner is up against when he sets about training a dog. In training a dog to obey commands, the owner is reinforcing that he is the top dog in the pack and that the dog should, and should want to, serve his superior. Thus, the owner is suppressing the dog's urge to dominate by modifying his behavior and making him obedient.

An important part of training is taking every opportunity to reinforce that you are the leader. The simple action of making your Great Dane sit to wait for his food says that you control when he eats and that he is dependent on you for food. Although it may be difficult, do not give in to your dog's wishes every time he whines at you or looks at you with his pleading eyes. It is a constant effort to show the dog that his

THE MIGHTY MALE

Males, whether castrated or not, will mount almost anything: a pillow, your leg or, much to your dismay, even your neighbor's leg. As with other types of inappropriate behavior, the dog must be corrected while in the act, which for once is not difficult. Often he will not let go! While a puppy is experimenting with his very first urges, his owners feel he needs to "sow his oats" and allow the pup to mount. As the pup grows into a full-size dog, with full-size urges, it becomes a nuisance and an embarrassment. Males always appear as if they are trying to "save the race," more determined and stronger than imaginable. While altering the dog at an appropriate age will limit the dog's desire, it usually does not remove it entirely.

place in the pack is at the bottom. This is not meant to sound cruel or inhumane. You love your Great Dane and you should treat him with care and affection. Dog training is not about being cruel, it is about molding the dog's behavior into what is acceptable and teaching him to live by your rules. In theory, it is quite simple: catch him in appropriate behavior and reward him for it. Add a dog into the equation and it becomes a bit more trying, but as a rule of thumb, positive reinforcement is what works best.

With a dominant dog, punishment and negative reinforcement can have the opposite effect of what you are after. It can make a dog fearful and/or act out aggressively if he feels he is being challenged. Remember, a dominant dog perceives himself at the top of the social heap and will fight to defend his perceived status. The best way to prevent that is never to give him reason to think that he is in control in the first place. If you are having trouble training your Great Dane and it seems as if he is constantly challenging your authority, seek the help of an obedience trainer or behavioral specialist. A professional will work with both you and your dog to teach you effective techniques to use at home. Beware of trainers who rely on excessively harsh methods; scolding is necessary now and then, but the focus in your training should *always* be on positive reinforcement.

SEXUAL BEHAVIOR

Dogs exhibit certain sexual behaviors that may have influenced your choice of male or female when you first purchased your Great Dane. To a certain extent, spaying/neutering will eliminate these behaviors, but if you are purchasing a dog that you wish to show or breed from, you should be aware of what you will have to deal with throughout your Great Dane's life.

Female dogs usually have two estruses per year, with each

season lasting about three weeks. These are the only times in which a female dog will mate, and she usually will not allow this until the second week of the cycle, but this does vary from bitch to bitch. If not bred during the heat cycle, it is not uncommon for a bitch to experience a false pregnancy, in which her mammary glands swell and she exhibits maternal tendencies toward toys or other objects.

Owners must also recognize that another common behavior, mounting, is not merely a sexual expression but also one of dominance. Be consistent and persistent in discouraging this behavior and you will find that you can "move mounters."

CHEWING

The national canine pastime is chewing! Every dog loves to sink his "canines" into a tasty bone, but just about anything will do! Dogs need to chew, to massage their gums, to make their new teeth feel better and to exercise their jaws. This is a natural behavior deeply embedded in all things canine. Your role as owner is not to stop the dog's chewing, but to redirect it to positive, chew-worthy objects. Be an informed owner and purchase proper chew toys like strong nylon bones that will not splinter. Be sure that the devices are safe and durable, since your dog's safety is at risk. Again, the owner is responsible

The Great Dane's powerful jaws can be very destructive if his chewing instincts are not directed toward something purposeful. Large durable chew devices are the key to keeping his teeth occupied and your possessions in one piece!

for ensuring a dog-proof environment. The best answer is prevention: that is, put your shoes, handbags and other tasty objects in their proper places (out of the reach of the growing canine mouth). Direct puppies to their toys whenever you see them tasting the furniture legs or the leg of your jeans. Make a loud noise to attract the pup's attention and immediately escort him to his chew toy and engage him with the toy for at least four minutes, praising and encouraging him all the while.

Some trainers recommend deterrents, such as hot pepper or another bitter spice or a product designed for this purpose, to discourage the dog from chewing unwanted objects. Test out these products with your dog before investing in a large quantity.

JUMPING UP

Jumping up is a dog's friendly way of saying hello! However friendly the greeting may be, the chances are that you and your visitors will not appreciate your dog's enthusiasm. A dog the size of the Great Dane is easily taller than many people when standing on his hind legs, and can just as easily knock someone over...even if the intention is good. With the Great Dane, it is best to discourage this behavior entirely, starting from puppyhood.

Pick a command such as "Off" (avoid using "Down" since you will use that for the dog to lie down) and tell him "Off" when he jumps up. Place him on the ground on all fours and have him sit, praising him the whole time. Always lavish him with praise and petting when he is in the sit position. That way you are still giving him a warm affectionate greeting, because you are just as pleased to see him as he is to see you!

DIGGING

Digging, which is seen as a destructive behavior to humans, is actually quite a natural behavior in dogs. Although your dog is not one of the "earth dogs" (also known as terriers, which are most commonly associated with digging), his desire to dig can be irrepressible and most frustrating. When digging occurs in your yard, it is actually a normal behavior redirected into something the dog can do in his everyday life. In the wild, a dog would be actively seeking food, making his own shelter, etc. He would be using his paws in a purposeful manner for his survival. Since you provide him with food and shelter, he has no need to use his paws for these purposes, and so the energy that he would be using may manifest itself in the form of craters all over your yard and flower beds.

Perhaps your dog is digging as a reaction to boredom—it is somewhat similar to someone eating a whole bag of chips in front of the TV—because they are there and there is not anything better to do! Basically, the answer is to provide the dog with adequate play and exercise so that his mind and paws are occupied, and so that he feels as if he is doing something useful.

Of course, digging is easiest to control if it is stopped as soon as possible, but it is often hard to catch a dog in the act. If your dog is a compulsive digger and is not easily distracted by other activities, you can designate an area on your property where it is okay for him to dig. If you catch him digging in an off-limits area of the garden, immediately bring him to the approved area and praise him for digging there. Keep a close eye on him so that you can catch him in the act—that is the only way to make him understand what is permitted and what is not. If you take him to a hole he dug an hour ago and tell him "No," he will understand that you are not fond of holes, dirt or flowers. If you catch him while he is stifle-deep in your tulips, that is when he will get your message.

BARKING

Dogs cannot talk—oh, what they would say if they could! Instead, barking is a dog's way of "talking." It can be somewhat frustrating because it is not always easy to tell what a dog means by his bark—is he excited, happy, frightened or angry? Whatever it is that the dog is trying to say, he should not be punished for barking. It is only when the barking becomes excessive, and when the excessive barking becomes a bad habit, that the behavior needs to be modified.

Fortunately, as superb watchdogs, Great Danes use their barks more purposefully than most other dogs. If an intruder came into your home in the middle of the night and your Great Dane barked a warning, wouldn't you be pleased? You would probably deem your dog a hero, a wonder-

QUIET ON THE SET
To encourage proper barking, you can teach your dog the command "Quiet." When someone comes to the door and the dog barks a few times, praise him. Talk to him soothingly and, when he stops barking, tell him "Quiet" and continue to praise him. In this sense, you are letting him bark his warning, which is an instinctive behavior, and then rewarding him for being quiet after a few barks. You may initially reward him with a treat after he has been quiet for a few minutes.

ful guardian and protector of the home. On the other hand, if a friend drops by unexpectedly and rings the doorbell and is greeted with a sudden sharp bark, you would probably be annoyed at the dog. But in reality, isn't this just the same behavior? The dog does not know any better...unless he sees who is at the door and it is someone he knows, he will bark as a means of vocalizing that his (and your) territory is being threatened. While your friend is not posing a threat, it is all the same to the dog. Barking is his means of letting you know that there is an intrusion, whether friend or foe, on your property. This type of barking is instinctive and should not be discouraged.

Excessive habitual barking, however, is a problem that should be corrected early on. As your

Great Dane grows up, you will be able to tell when his barking is purposeful and when it is for no reason. You will become able to distinguish your dog's different barks and their meanings. For example, the bark when someone comes to the door will be different than the bark when he is excited to see you. It is similar to a person's tone of voice, except that the dog has to rely totally on tone of voice because he does not have the benefit of using words. An incessant barker will be evident at an early age.

There are some things that encourage a dog to bark. For example, if your dog barks non-stop for a few minutes and you give him a treat to quiet him, he believes that you are rewarding him for barking. He will associate barking with getting a treat and will keep doing it until he is rewarded.

FOOD STEALING

Is your dog devising ways of stealing food from your table or pantry? If so, you must answer the following questions: Is your Great Dane hungry, or is he "constantly famished" like many dogs seem to be? Face it, some dogs are more food-motivated than others. Some dogs are totally obsessed by the smell of food and can only think of their next meal. Food stealing is terrific fun and always yields a great reward—food, glorious food.

The owner's goal, therefore, is to be sensible about where food is placed in the home, and to reprimand your dog whenever he is caught in the act of stealing. But remember, only reprimand the dog if you actually catch him stealing, not later when the crime is discovered, for that will be of no use at all and will only serve to confuse.

BEGGING

Just like food stealing, begging is a favorite pastime of hungry puppies! It yields that same great reward—food! Dogs quickly learn that their owners keep the "good food" for themselves, and that humans do not dine on dried food alone. Begging is a conditioned response related to a specific stimulus, time and place. The sounds of the kitchen, cans and bottles opening, crinkling bags, the smell of food in preparation, etc., will excite the dog and soon the paws are in the air!

Here is the solution to stopping this behavior: Never give in to a beggar! You are rewarding the dog for sitting pretty, jumping up, whining and rubbing his nose into you by giving him that glorious reward—food. By ignoring the dog, you will (eventually) force the behavior into extinction. Note that the behavior is likely to get worse before it disappears, so be sure there are not any "softies" in the family who will give in to

"Oliver" every time he whimpers "More, please."

SEPARATION ANXIETY

Your Great Dane may howl, whine or otherwise vocalize his displeasure at your leaving the house and his being left alone. This is a normal reaction, no different than the child who cries as his mother leaves him on the first day at school. However, separation anxiety is more serious and can lead to destructive behavior. Obviously, you enjoy spending time with your dog, and he thrives on your love and attention. However, it should not become a dependent relationship in which he is heartbroken without you.

One thing you can do to minimize separation anxiety is to make your entrances and exits as low-key as possible. Do not give your dog a long drawn-out goodbye, and do not lavish him with hugs and kisses when you return. This is giving in to the attention that he craves, and it will only make him miss it more when you are away. Another thing you can try is to give your dog a treat when you leave; this not only will keep him occupied and keep his mind off the fact that you have just left but also will help him associate your leaving with a pleasant experience.

You may have to accustom your dog to being left alone in intervals. Of course, when your

dog starts whimpering as you approach the door, your first instinct will be to run to him and comfort him, but do not do it! Eventually he will adjust and be just fine if you take it in small steps. His anxiety stems from being placed in an unfamiliar situation; by familiarizing him with being alone, he will learn that he is okay. That is not to say you should purposely leave your dog home alone, but the dog needs to know that while he can depend on you for his care, you do not have to be by his side 24 hours a day.

When the dog is alone in the house, he should be confined to his designated dog-proof area of the house. This should be the area in which he sleeps and already feels comfortable so he will feel more at ease when he is alone.

Don't expect your dog to resist temptation when food is involved—if there's food within the dog's reach, it's fair game as far as he's concerned!

INDEX

My Great Dane

PUT YOUR PUPPY'S FIRST PICTURE HERE

Dog's Name _____

Date _____ Photographer _____